THE AMERICAN TRADITION IN
RELIGION AND EDUCATION

The American Tradition in Religion and Education

By

R. FREEMAN BUTTS

GREENWOOD PRESS, PUBLISHERS
WESTPORT, CONNECTICUT

Library of Congress Cataloging in Publication Data

Butts, Robert Freeman, 1910-
  The American tradition in religion and education.

  Reprint of the ed. published by Beacon Press, Boston,
in series: Beacon Press studies in freedom and power.
  Includes bibliographical references.
  1. Church and State in the United States.
2. Church and education in the United States.
I. Title.
[BR516.B85 1974]   261.7'0973   73-20903
ISBN 0-8371-5875-3

Reprinted by arrangement with Beacon Press and the
American Humanist Association

Reprinted in 1974 by Greenwood Press,
a division of Williamhouse-Regency Inc.

Library of Congress Catalog Card Number 73-20903

ISBN 0-8371-5875-3

Printed in the United States of America

Foreword

THIS VOLUME is sponsored by the Institute of Church and State, a non-profit corporation of the State of New York organized for the purpose of encouraging and distributing objective and scholarly studies respecting the relation of church and state in education. The Institute deems the educational aspect of the relation of church and state to be an exceedingly important phase of the democratic tradition of our country and as such worthy of most serious study by all who would uphold democracy and support and upbuild the American tradition.

The Institute counts itself fortunate to be able to offer, as its first sponsored volume of research, *The American Tradition in Religion and Education*. The author, Professor R. Freeman Butts, is eminently fitted for his task. He is an outstanding authority in the history of education. His scholarly works are granted first rank. He has for years been conducting research in the area treated. The Institute believes that this volume constitutes the most thorough, careful, and trustworthy study yet made in the specific area covered. It is but fair to both to add that the author, not the Institute, is responsible for the positions taken in the work.

V. T. THAYER
Chairman

Contents

Preface

THE AMERICAN PEOPLE are once more engaged in a great debate over the proper relationship between church and state. It is an old debate, one that has been going on ever since the first colonists came to these shores; yet to each successive generation it always seems to be new. Today the issue centers in large part upon schools and education. As such, it is a question that touches some of the deepest convictions of the American people. Religious beliefs, democratic values, and the education of children always raise sharp differences of opinion, but when all of these three are joined together and focussed on one problem, the debate readily becomes fired with emotion and beset with confusion. More than ever before Americans need sound and straight thinking to see their way through the conflicting demands and counter-demands, the charges and counter-charges that arise over questions of religion, government, and education.

Wherever one looks, the debate is going on: in the halls of Congress and state legislatures, in public hearings and in private homes, in political campaigns and party platforms, in court rooms and in pulpits, in schools and colleges, in a flood of newspaper and magazine articles, pamphlets, and books. Manifestos, policy statements, and demands for legislation are being made by all kinds of formal and informal groups, religious, political, professional, labor, business, patriotic, and civic. Since the end of the Second World War, the debate has become increasingly widespread and often touched with bitterness.

This book is not another manifesto nor another proposal for action. It is designed to provide the historical perspective upon which to base sound public policy. It is addressed to the teaching profession, school administrators, religious leaders, public officials, and all citizens who are concerned with religion and education. All individuals and groups make their decisions on the basis of some judgment of history, more or less consciously formulated, and many use historical arguments to justify their proposals. The purpose of this book is to present the historical evidence that should be taken into account when present decisions are made. It is intended to provide historical guide-lines against which to measure the validity of current proposals. It asks the questions of the historical materials that people should now be asking as they carry on the great debate. It does not presume to give final or dogmatic answers. It is hoped that it will contribute to the strengthening and widening of the reasoned and sober elements in the present discussions and thus will serve in some measure to lessen the asperities of the controversy.

Times of great stress or social conflict produce a tendency to rewrite history or at least to reinterpret it in such way that it can be made to support one's favorite position. Everyone likes to have history on his side. The rewriting of history, if done without due regard to sound historical scholarship, can be a vicious perversion of truth and justice in the interests of partisan or national crusading. This approach can lead to the adulations and absurdities of totalitarian history writing, the results of which are so familiar in fascist, nazi, and communist posturing of recent years. These are desecrations of the liberal and democratic ideal of historical objectivity that has long been a mainstay of the method of intelligence.

There is another sense, however, and a legitimate sense, in which history needs to be reassessed by each generation in the light of the prevailing issues and dominant concerns of the times but always with a loyalty and respect for the accepted canons of scholarship. Historical "facts" do not just lie around waiting to be picked up. History does not write itself independently of the outlook and point of view of the historian. The historian looks at the documentary materials of the past through the eyes of his time and place and with consciousness of the critical problems that press upon his contemporaries for decision. History writing should avoid the purely antiquarian interests of sterile logic-chopping as well as the devious manipulations of biased propaganda. Its main task is to re-examine the past in the light of present problems as an aid to deciding what should be done in the future.

Most participants in the present debate over church and state are claiming that they are loyal to the historic principle of separation of church and state and that our historic tradition of separation supports their cause. There are those who desire that sectarian religious instruction be promoted by the public schools or who desire that public funds be used for services to children in non-public and religious schools. They claim that the true meaning of the American tradition supports their desires for these kinds of "co-operation" between church and state. Opposed to this position are those who claim that history supports their contentions that religious instruction should not be promoted by the public schools and that public funds should not be used for religious schools. They argue that such "co-operation" is really an entanglement that amounts to fusion or alliance between church and state. Can both be right? Or is the meaning of our history so clear that only one side may appropriately use the historical argument to support its claims? This book seeks to answer these questions on the basis of the most authentic historical evidence available.

On the other hand, there are those on both sides of the debate who do not put much stock in the historical argument. They either do not care what the history means or they believe that the historical evidence may support the other side. In either case, they argue that no matter what history shows the American people should decide the issues only on the present merits of their case or on the basis of conditions that have appeared since the early battles over church and state were fought. Such persons may or may not be persuaded by the historical evidence presented in the following pages, but they would do well not to underestimate the potency of the historical argument.

This book is written on the assumption that the historical argument does make a difference in our present decisions. It argues that many of our present controversies are the result of divergent historical traditions that persist among us. People act and think as they do in large part because of the inherited values and ideals that live on in them as traditions. When these traditions come into conflict, we are faced with unresolved problems in the present. Wise resolution of these problems will take account of our historical traditions. Nowhere is this more evident than in the great debate over religion and education. If present decisions are to be made with a maximum of intelligence and reason and a minimum of propaganda or sheer struggle for power, then decisions should be made upon a sound interpretation of the past. We court disaster if we ignore the living traditions of our people.

It is within this framework that the history of the relations between church and state in America has been re-examined in this book. Until recently most historians have concentrated in their writings on the struggle for "the free exercise" of religion. Now, however, the general agreement is that the free exercise of religion is an accepted and desirable part of the American way of life.

The issue in education today centers not so much upon whether religious freedom is desirable, as on whether it can be maintained if the state gives support or aid to religious schools or if religious instruction becomes a part of the program of the public schools. This raises the question concerning the meaning of "an establishment of religion" as stated in the First Amendment of the Constitution and as embodied in the several state constitutions. Does the ban on "an establishment of religion" prohibit "co-operation" between church and state in education or is greater "co-operation" than we now have both permissible and desirable? Does "co-operation" amount to an alliance or fusion of church and state?

As a result, historians are looking again at the record of the past to discover the authentic meaning of "an establishment of religion." When this search is conducted in the midst of a great debate, the search can be fascinating and exciting, provided one is not carried away by his desires to find what he is hoping he will find. The canons of scholarship will not allow perversion of the record or hiding of significant parts of it. However, the historian cannot bring to bear all of the records of the past, and thus he must select only the materials that are relevant and pertinent to the issue at hand. This selection will inevitably reflect a frame of reference or a set of values that may or may not be consciously admitted. The careful historian must be aware of his own assumptions and values, and he should state them for all to see and judge. If the canons of scholarship have been observed, if the historian's point of view is open for inspection and criticism, and if the reader may then judge whether or not the historian's evidence supports his conclusions in the light of his point of view, the values of objectivity have been preserved.

This book is frankly written in a framework of values which includes the following assumptions: that religious freedom is a foundation stone of American liberty, that the preservation of the equal rights of religious conscience is a necessity for genuine religious freedom, that the guarantee of religious freedom is an essential function of our constitutional form of government, that public education is a bulwark of our common democratic values, that private education has a legitimate and desirable function to serve in American society, and that "an establishment of religion" (as defined in Chapters 2, 3, and 4) is a threat to religious freedom and to the American tradition of democracy. This all means, by and large, that the historic principle of separation of church and state as defined in 175 years of American history is a desirable tradition to maintain in American education (as outlined in Chapters 5 and 6). These are the working hypotheses upon which the investigation in this book has been undertaken. Whether or not the conclusions reached are justifiable depends in the last analysis upon public judgment.

Therefore, this book should be rigorously put to the following tests: its adherence to the historical facts and accurate use of the documents; its comprehensiveness in using the documents so that pertinent evidence is not overlooked or taken out of context; the inclusiveness and validity of its frame of reference as judged by democratic ends and values; and the validity of its interpretations of the historical evidence and their meaning for the present debate. In these ways this book must be judged by the community of competent historical scholars and, above all, by the practical intelligence of the American people as a whole. If it is vulnerable in any of these respects, it should be corrected by competent criticism. If it stands the test, it should be useful in the making of sound public policy.

R. FREEMAN BUTTS

Teachers College
Columbia University

THE AMERICAN TRADITION IN
RELIGION AND EDUCATION

1

The Choices Before Us

UNTIL RECENT YEARS few Americans questioned the assumption that one of our nation's most firmly established traditions was the principle of the separation of church and state. Children have long been taught in our schools that many early colonists and later immigrants came to America to escape the religious persecutions of Europe and to gain here the opportunity to worship freely and believe as they saw fit. We have gloried in this tradition of religious freedom and found in it a continuing source of renewal for our faith in American democracy as against any kind of tyranny or totalitarianism.

In recent years, however, conscientious Americans of different faiths have become increasingly troubled in their efforts to decide what the principle of separation means in practice. Men of good will and integrity have begun to differ markedly in their outlooks, especially when confronted with what "separation" means with respect to education. For example, demands have been made that religious schools should have a share in public tax funds along with the public schools; and it has been claimed that this would not violate the principle of separation of church and state, properly understood. The conscientious citizen of any faith might well ask, "If in practice we may allocate tax funds to sectarian schools without violating the principle of separation of church and state, what *does* the principle mean?"

3

Likewise, a chorus of voices has been raised asking for more direct religious instruction in the public schools and at the same time affirming belief in the principle of separation of church and state. The conscientious and loyal citizen, thinking he believes in the principle of separation, might well ask, "*Does* religious instruction in the public schools violate the principle of separation? If not, what does separation mean?" Similarly, the practice of releasing children from public school hours to receive religious instruction from their own religious teachers has been advocated and defended on the grounds that it does not violate the principle of separation of church and state. Many Americans have thought released time to be a desirable practice, and they wonder what all the objection to it can possibly be. "*Does* released time violate the principle of separation?"

Such questions as these have become increasingly difficult to answer for Americans who have both the welfare of religion and of public education at heart. The storm of controversy that has been raised over two recent Supreme Court decisions has added to the confusion and uncertainty in the minds of many citizens.[1]

In the Everson case the majority of the Supreme Court in a 5 to 4 decision ruled that the use of public tax funds in New Jersey to reimburse parents for the transportation of their children to parochial schools is constitutional and does not violate the principle of separation of church and state as set forth in the First Amendment of the United States Constitution. In the McCollum case the Supreme Court ruled 8 to 1 that the practice of releasing children from public school time for religious instruction in public school buildings is unconstitutional because it violates the same principle of separation of church and state as defined in the First Amendment. Many persons have felt that the principle of separation as defined by the court was consistent in both cases but that

[1]References are to Notes at the end of the book.

the court contradicted itself when it came to apply the principle in practice to these two cases.

Now the confusion has been worse confounded because other persons have begun to raise questions about the principle of separation itself.[2] From this point of view it is argued that the whole point of our historical tradition has been misunderstood and that the American people never intended to "separate" church from state but simply to distinguish between their functions in such way as to prevent the establishment of a single national church, to assure religious freedom, and to facilitate "co-operation" between church and state. In other words, this view argues that it is a mistake to think that America has ever had a well-defined *principle* of separation of church and state. On this basis it is easy to argue that the use of public funds for sectarian schools, religious instruction in public schools, and released time are perfectly proper examples of the principle of "co-operation" between church and state.

In view of the confusion arising out of such practices in education and in view of the attacks upon the principle of separation of church and state, it is imperative that Americans become aware once more of the historical tradition which we have been led to cherish but the original meaning of which we may have forgotten. If there is an authentic tradition of separation of church and state which we should value highly, then we should understand it clearly as one basis for deciding such practical issues as have been cited. If there is no such authentic tradition or if the original meaning is no longer valid, then we are free to decide the practical issues of the present without regard to the original aims and purposes of that tradition in the past. *But we should know what we are doing.*

This book is an effort to state as clearly, as briefly, and as objectively as possible what the weight of historical evidence means concerning the American principle and practice of separation of church and state. It does not pretend to rest upon any exhaustive original investigations of its own, but it does rely for the most part upon original documents and draws upon the most competent and verifiable historical scholarship available. When faced with the necessity of making such important decisions of policy as these, the public will not find ready-made answers in the past. In other words, history will not give us the answers for the future, but intelligent decisions will take account of the vital traditions that live on in us. In our present and future decisions we ignore the past at our peril.

In the pages that follow, a portion of the available historical evidence is presented in order to help the American people decide whether or not the principle of separation of church and state is an authentic and valid tradition in America. It has been widely agreed that the principle of separation has had two integrally related aspects, both of which are essential to its meaning. Relying upon the words of the First Amendment most Americans have assumed that our tradition means, first, that government shall "make no law respecting an establishment of religion"; and it means, in the second place, that the government shall make no law "prohibiting the free exercise" of religion.

It is the purpose here to bring these phrases and their historical meanings under careful scrutiny as a means of clarifying the choices that lie before us. To repeat, separation of church and state in America has meant "no establishment of religion" and it has meant "free exercise of religion." It is, of course, possible for the American people to propose that we modify or combine these two concepts in one or more ways. Theoretically, four possible combinations might be made; they represent the choices before the American people:

(1) *No establishment of religion; no free exercise of religion.* We could destroy religious freedom without returning to religious establishments. If we did so we would move

in the direction of recent totalitarian attacks upon religion as exemplified in Nazi Germany and, more recently, in the Communist countries of Eastern Europe. Democracy is surely committed to opposing all such proposals with all the force at its disposal. Our democracy could not include government hostility toward any religious belief or church as such, for free exercise of religion is plainly a part of our Bill of Rights as contained in the national and state constitutions.

(2) *"Co-operation" between church and state with no religious freedom (single establishment; no free exercise of religion).* We could try to depart from both meanings of separation and return to an establishment of religion and at the same time destroy free exercise of religion. This would return us to something like the systems represented by the non-Christian state religions of Imperial Rome, or the Holy Roman Empire in medieval times, or the Church of England in Reformation England and colonial Virginia, or the Puritan theocracy of colonial New England.

In these systems the force of law was used to promote "co-operation" of the state with a single church by giving it protection and support while at the same time outlawing and penalizing all other religious beliefs and practices. These were the standing orders established in certain American colonies in the seventeenth century (see Chapter 2). Few serious proposals are being made today by responsible groups in America to achieve this end. Democracy could not permit the establishment of a single state religion, any more than it could destroy free exercise of religion and still live within the framework or spirit of the First Amendment of the United States Constitution and of the state constitutions.

(3) *"Co-operation" between church and state with some freedom of religion.* A third alternative would be to re-

establish religion by law but at the same time try to maintain free exercise of religion. This was the compromise that was tried in America in the eighteenth century as the dissenting sects began to demand religious freedom for themselves in the face of the established churches. This compromise took two forms:

(a) *Single establishment with free exercise.* The attempt was made to maintain one church as the established religion of the state but to tolerate and permit public worship by other religious groups. This was more or less reluctantly granted by the established orders during the eighteenth century (see Chapter 2). Some groups may view this as an ultimate ideal to be achieved in America, but few would proclaim it to be possible of achievement in the near future.

(b) *Multiple establishment with free exercise.* As the dissenting groups became ever stronger in the later eighteenth century, a second stage of compromise was tried whereby several or many religious groups were admitted to the privileges of aid and support by the state. In this phase of compromise it was hoped that the older establishments could be saved from complete separation by having the state support many or all religions equally or impartially. This objective is now being seriously proposed by different religious groups as the proper relationship of "co-operation" between church and state in America.

This is being described as the authentic American tradition and thus not contrary to the First Amendment. Actually, however, as will be shown in Chapters 3 and 4, it is this very system which was prohibited by the national and state constitutions of the American people in the late eighteenth and early nineteenth centuries as they moved to create a new society on this continent. They came to believe that genuine religious freedom could not be achieved while maintaining any legal connection between the state and any one or any number of churches.

(4) *Separation of church and state (no single or multiple establishment; complete freedom of religion).* Upon realizing that choices two and three both included some form of establishment, Americans moved to a fourth solution, namely, religious freedom with no single or multiple establishment of religion by law. This is the principle of separation of church and state as developed in the late eighteenth and early nineteenth centuries (see Chapters 3 and 4). This alternative has been enacted in the Constitution of the United States and in the constitutions of the several states.

Since the first alternative has not been an authentic part of the American tradition, it will not be dealt with further here, but it is the purpose of the following pages to describe as fairly as possible how the other three alternatives have been tried in America. Roughly, they appeared in chronological order over the period of three hundred years.

The main point at issue for most conscientious Americans is whether "co-operation" or "separation" embodies the most desirable American tradition of the relations between church and state. The vast majority of Americans are agreed on maintaining free exercise of religion, and they are agreed in opposing establishment of a single religion. The genuine issue, therefore, for most Americans narrows down to a choice between (3b) or (4), to a choice between "co-operation" of the state with many churches or full separation of church and state.

Those who favor multiple "co-operation" say that "no

establishment of religion" means simply that no single church may be established but that the state is free to encourage and "co-operate" with all churches just so long as it treats them all impartially and fairly. This co-operative relationship is also referred to as "functional interaction" or "mutual support and aid" or "harmony."

Those who favor "separation" say that "no establishment of religion" means that there shall be no legal connection between the state and any one or all churches and, further, that this does *not* mean state hostility toward religion but is the basic *condition* of genuine religious freedom. Adherents of this view argue that "co-operation" as defined above is really an "entanglement" and will lead in the future, as in the past, to "an establishment of religion." The meaning of "establishment of religion" thus becomes critical for any sound decision involving the relation of church and state in American education (see Chapters 5 and 6).

2

What "Establishment of Religion" Meant in Colonial America

As AMERICANS FACE such choices as the foregoing, they will hear more and more of the somewhat unfamiliar phrase "establishment of religion." Even though these words may be unfamiliar today they had full and specific meaning for the American colonies. The phrase should become widely familiar again as we re-examine our past to recapture the original meaning of our tradition of church and state.

This tradition is stated for the nation at large in the words of the First Amendment of the United States Constitution: "Congress shall make no law respecting an establishment of religion, nor prohibiting the free exercise thereof." The first task, then, is to try to define the specific meanings attached by the American colonists to the words "an establishment of religion."

SINGLE ESTABLISHMENTS

A full understanding of these words requires a look at the various conceptions of the relation between church and state which were current in Europe at the time of the founding of America. In the sixteenth and seventeenth centuries the various Protestant groups waged their battles to break the hold of the Roman Catholic Church in Europe by relying upon the rising national states for financial, military, and moral support. The major religious settlements were thus basically political settlements. In Germany the religion of the people of the various states was to be determined by the civil rulers; in England the crown became the head of the Church of England in place of the Pope in Rome; in Geneva John Calvin used the civil authority to enforce his conception of true religion.

The major Protestant groups of the sixteenth century became close allies of the civil state in various ways. Despite the differences in this relationship all these major Protestant churches had in common the fact that they were religions established by law. Thus, "establishment of religion" represented the basic Reformation doctrine that the welfare of the state required the state to sponsor and support an authorized religion, because it was believed that dissenting or heretical beliefs were a danger to civil society as well as a danger to the "true" religion, whatever it happened to be. Thus, "co-operation" was an integral part of establishment from the beginning.

In the medieval conception of church and state the Roman Church was asserted to have authority over the spiritual and eternal welfare of the people, and the state was to exert authority over the temporal and civil welfare of the same people. The church and state were, however, to "co-operate" in their joint mission to achieve a Christian community on earth. Both church and state were conceived as corporate entities receiving their authority from God, each with its own defined sphere of action. But the Church maintained that, inasmuch as it dealt with supernatural affairs while the state dealt with natural affairs, the Church was obviously superior to the state whenever matters of controversy or conflict arose between church and state.

This doctrine had long been stated by the medieval church but nowhere more clearly and directly than in the bull *Unam Sanctam* issued in 1302 by Pope Boniface VIII:

. . . there is one holy catholic and apostolic church, outside of which there is neither salvation nor remission of sins; . . . In this church there is one Lord, one faith, and one baptism. . . . Therefore of this one and only church there is one body and one head — not two heads as if it were a monster: — Christ, namely, and the vicar of Christ, St. Peter, and the successor of Peter. . . . We are told by the word of the gospel that in this His fold there are two swords, — a spiritual, namely, and a temporal. . . . Both swords, the spiritual and the material, therefore, are in the power of the church; the one, indeed, to be wielded for the church, the other by the church; the one by the hand of the priest, the other by the hand of kings and knights, but at the will and sufferance of the priest. One sword, moreover, ought to be under the other, and the temporal authority to be subjected to the spiritual . . . that the spiritual exceeds any earthly power in dignity and nobility we ought the more openly to confess the more spiritual things excel temporal ones. . . . For, the truth bearing witness, the spiritual power has to establish the earthly power, and to judge it if it be not good.[1]

The functions of church and state were to be distinct, but they were to co-operate in achieving the public welfare as well as maintaining the true religion. The Church defined heresy, and the state punished the heretics. The state often gave financial support to the clergy because the Church was considered to be a concern of the whole community rather than simply a concern of those individuals who desired to support the Church. Of course, the rulers of the rising national states did not always agree with this version of the proper relations of church and state nor did some of the Holy Roman Emperors who were sworn to defend the faith.

In those national states where the Roman Church was overthrown, the various Protestant religions were established by law in place of the Catholic religion. In some German states and in Scandanavia Lutheranism was established; in the Netherlands the Reformed Church was established; in England the Church of England was established; in Geneva Calvinism was established; in Scotland Presbyterianism was established. In all these cases it was assumed that religion was a concern of the whole community and hence should be supported by the state.

Thus the idea of co-operation between church and state survived the Protestant Revolution and was accepted alike by Catholic and Protestant governments. Uniformity, at least in the outward manifestations of religion, was generally regarded as essential to national unity.[2]

In order to see even more clearly what "establishment of religion" meant to the early colonists in America, it is necessary to describe briefly the character of the two major forms of establishment in America, first, the Church of England which was carried to Virginia and to several other American colonies, and, second, the Calvinism which was carried by the Puritans to New England.

The Anglican Establishment

The Church of England became the established church in England as a result of a long series of conflicts with Rome; the changes in the relationship between church and state were embodied in the legal enactments of Parliament under Henry VIII, Edward VI, and Elizabeth. The English crown displaced the Pope as the supreme head of the church; the crown controlled all appointments of bishops, gave permission to the church bodies to meet, and regulated the doctrine and the procedures of church worship. The Act of Uniformity of Parliament required the Book of Common Prayer to be the only legal form of public worship and fixed penalties for clergymen who did not follow the orders set down therein.

Opposition to the articles of faith or to the methods of public worship constituted a breach of civil law and could be punished by the civil authorities. The state required attendance at church, prohibited public worship by dissenters, prohibited dissenters from holding public office, and punished offenders in any of these respects. In the local parishes the minister, the wardens, and the vestrymen had certain civil authority as well as religious privileges. They supervised attendance at church which was required of all persons whether or not they wished to adhere to the Church of England, and they enforced laws concerning poor relief, hunting, vagrancy, and drunkenness. All persons were forced to pay taxes for the support of the parish church, no matter what their own religious beliefs might be.

This system of establishment was carried in substance to Virginia where the commercial company in charge was authorized by the royal charter of 1606 to give financial support to ministers, require church attendance of all settlers, and levy penalties upon any who spoke blasphemy or heresy. Virginia thus followed in essence the pattern from the homeland. When the commercial company's charter was taken away and Virginia was made into a royal province in 1624, a full-fledged Anglican establishment was soon put into effect by acts of the Virginia Assembly beginning in 1629.

Without attempting to describe details, it may be said that "establishment" in Virginia clearly meant the following things:

(1) It meant that the state enforced *financial support* for the established church. The state levied taxes in the form of tithes upon all persons without regard to their religious beliefs, and these taxes or tithes were enforced by law for the support of the parish clergymen. Church buildings were often built with the aid of tax funds and public lands. In addition, certain lands (called the glebes) were set aside for the clergy who were entitled to such lands by law as a means for their support either for income or for actual residence.

(2) Establishment also meant that the state gave *legal and*

moral support to the doctrines and public worship of the established church. The state prohibited the free exercise of religion and legislated against equal rights of conscience. No religious beliefs except the legally approved religion could be stated publicly or taught publicly without danger of legal punishment by the state. The laws required all clergymen to conform to the doctrines and methods of worship of the Church of England. Clergymen who failed to conform were banished by state action, and certain non-conformists were singled out for special legal action, including Puritans, Quakers, Baptists, and Catholics who were subject to fines, imprisonment, or expulsion. Not only was the free exercise of worship by non-conformists prohibited by law, but also all persons regardless of religious belief were required by law to attend the services of the Church of England with fines and penalties for failure to do so. In the local parishes the church officials (wardens and vestrymen) undertook such civil tasks as enforcing the laws respecting parish taxes, apprenticeship of orphans, and administration of poor relief.[3]

In brief, establishment meant that the Church of England not only received legal privileges of public worship and faith which were accorded to no other belief, but also the compulsive and legal force of the state was used to enforce these privileges and to support the clergy and property of the established church by aid of lands and taxes. To give effect to these principles the legislature passed many laws "respecting an establishment of religion" as well as "prohibiting the free exercise thereof." Somewhat similar forms of Anglican establishment were enacted in the Carolinas and eventually in Maryland and Georgia. This form of single establishment was one kind of "co-operation" between church and state which the American people sought to prevent when they began the long struggle toward separation of church and state in the eighteenth century.

The Puritan Establishment

The English Puritans followed in general John Calvin's doctrines in their efforts to reform the Church of England and also to counteract the "radical" Protestant sects who wanted free exercise of religion and separation of church and state. Despite Calvin's great hostility to the Roman Church, his position was somewhat similar to that of the Catholic Church regarding the relation of church and state. He insisted that the church should be supreme in religious affairs and that it was the obligation of the state to enforce the church's pronouncements on religion. The church was thus superior to the state in Calvin's Geneva experiment, but the two were to co-operate in enforcement.

This doctrine is nowhere more explicitly stated than in Calvin's basic theological work of 1536 entitled the *Institutes of the Christian Religion;* the civil government must not confine itself to secular affairs, but its first aim is to support the true religion:

> . . . civil government is designed, as long as we live in this world, to cherish and support the external worship of God, to preserve the pure doctrine of religion, to defend the constitution of the Church, to regulate our lives in a manner requisite for the society of men, to form our manners to civil justice, to promote our concord with each other, and to establish general peace and tranquility; . . . .
> . . . its objects also are, that idolatry, sacrileges against the name of God, blasphemies against his truth, and other offences against religion, may not openly appear and be disseminated among the people; . . . in short, that there may be a public form of religion among Christians, and that humanity may be maintained among men . . . .
> . . . no government can be happily constituted, unless its first

object be the promotion of piety and . . . all laws are preposterous which neglect the claims of God, and merely provide for the interests of men. Therefore, as religion holds the first place among all the philosophers, and as this has always been regarded by the universal consent of all nations, Christian princes and magistrates ought to be ashamed of their indolence, if they do not make it the object of their most serious care. We have already shown that this duty is particularly enjoined upon them by God; for it is reasonable that they should employ their utmost efforts in asserting and defending the honor of him, whose vicegerents they are, and by whose favor they govern. . . . These things evince the folly of those who would wish magistrates to neglect all thoughts of God, and to confine themselves entirely to the administration of justice among men; as though God appointed governors in his name to decide secular controversies, and disregarded that which is of far greater importance — the pure worship of himself according to the rule of his law.[4]

On this basis the Puritans in England could not accept the Anglican doctrine that the civil ruler in the person of the crown was the supreme authority in religious affairs. They were not by any means arguing for separation of church and state. They simply wanted to be sure that the state enforced the orthodox religion as defined by the Puritan church.

Puritans agreed with the Roman Church and with the Anglican Church that morality must rest upon religious sanctions and to that end the church and state should co-operate, but they wanted to be sure that the Roman Church did not have the right to define this co-operation, and they wanted to be sure that the state as conceived by the Anglican settlement did not have the right to define this co-operation. They agreed that the welfare of the community depended upon the establishment of orthodox religion, but they were convinced that the establishment of either the Catholic or Anglican religion by the state would destroy rather than promote the secular welfare of civil society. Thus, the civil welfare, in the view of all three churches, depended upon the establishment by authority of the state of a specific view of religious orthodoxy.

The public welfare would be endangered if any other religious view were allowed to be held or taught openly among the people.

Thus, when the Puritans came to New England one of their primary concerns was to establish their own religious orthodoxy as the law of the land in Massachusetts, Connecticut, and New Hampshire. In many ways they showed their intent that the state should support the Congregational Church in accordance with Calvin's outlook. In Massachusetts, suffrage was even restricted to church members as well as to property holders in the effort to be sure that no unorthodox influence should be exerted in civil affairs. The principle of "co-operation" between church and state was fully in operation in the full meaning of the Puritan Congregational establishment.

(1) The state levied taxes for the support of the clergy and the church.

(2) The state enforced by law the exclusive rights of the orthodox church to conduct public worship and to compel all persons to attend church services no matter what their beliefs.

(3) The state used its coercive power to deny equal rights to the unorthodox. Not only were they denied political rights, they were subject to trial and punishment by the state for heresy, blasphemy, and idolatry, and, to a lesser extent, even for criticizing the ministers. Roger Williams, Anne Hutchinson, Presbyterians, Quakers, Anabaptists, and Catholics all felt the force of the Puritan civil authorities in trials, fines, banishment, or punishment.

Thus, in summary, to colonial Americans of the seventeenth century the term "establishment of religion" meant two things in principle and in practice. It meant *positive support of religion by public funds,* and it meant *legal enforcement of certain orthodox religious beliefs* by granting to certain churches the exclusive privileges of public worship as well as by meting out punishment for those who tried to conduct other kinds of public worship or even to hold privately religious beliefs at variance with the established religion. This, then, is the original meaning of the second choice before the American people as described on page 7. Co-operation without free exercise was the dominant principle and practice brought from Europe to the Anglican South and to Puritan New England in the seventeenth century.

When Americans began to move away from this meaning of establishment, they discovered that the process would not be complete until they had removed the legal obligation to give financial support to religious doctrines in which they did not believe and until they had removed from the state the right to enforce modes of worship upon all or to penalize persons for unorthodox beliefs. In other words, they had to *disestablish financial and legal connection* between state and church; and they had to gain recognition of the *rights of all to exercise freely* their own modes of worship. They found that both of these steps had to be taken before they could achieve the principle that all persons have *equal rights of conscience* in the eyes of the state. Prior to the Revolutionary War most of the gains toward separation of church and state were made in the realm of free exercise of religion rather than in direct progress toward financial or legal disestablishment.

THE STRUGGLE FOR "FREE EXERCISE" OF RELIGION

From the foregoing descriptions it is clear that one of the dominant traditions in early colonial America was the acceptance of the principle that church and state were legitimate partners in the propagation and maintenance of an established religion. It should be noted immediately, however, that a second and equally authentic tradition was present in America from almost the beginning. This was the tradition of "separatism" which began as a minority viewpoint in the early seventeenth century but which became a majority point of view toward the end of the eighteenth century. As the tradition of separatism won its way in principle, the practice of establishment began to crumble on many fronts, until a high degree of separation was eventually won.

The theory of separation of church and state, or separatism, as it may conveniently be called, had its roots among some of the smaller Protestant sects of Europe in the sixteenth and seventeenth centuries. Among the most important of these, the Anabaptists of Switzerland, southern Germany, and the Low Countries resisted any civil or ecclesiastical authority that tried to enforce uniformity of belief. Thus, to achieve freedom of conscience for themselves and for others they fought against any union of church and state. They argued that all churches were voluntary associations of believers, and therefore they could brook no interference of the civil power with ecclesiastical affairs. Since religion must be an individual relationship between each individual and God, they said, any coercion upon individuals is sinful and useless; the state must confine itself to civil affairs and leave religion to religious agencies.   Baptists and Mennonites later reflected much of the original Anabaptist outlook.

Perhaps the most effective early statement of the principle of separation of church and state was made by Roger Williams in the course of his bitter conflict with the Massachusetts authorities under the leadership of the Puritan clergyman John Cotton. Williams went much beyond the theory of toleration that was being proposed by John Locke and others in England. Williams believed that conflict between various religions could end only when there was essential separation between church and state, when the legal connections between civil and religious authorities were cut away. Civil authorities have their secular sphere and religious authorities have their religious sphere; neither should try to control the affairs of the other. All religious beliefs should not only be allowed freedom to exist but the state must not infringe the *equal* rights of any religious belief, Christian or non-Christian. He even held that freedom of *non-belief* should be allowed by the state. He believed that only in these ways may the true welfare of the state as well as of all religions be achieved.

Certain excerpts from the preface of Williams' famous tract entitled *Bloudy Tenent of Persecution* are important in this connection:

Fourthly, The *Doctrine of persecution* for cause of *Conscience,* is proved guilty of all the *blood* of the *Soules* crying for *vengeance* under the *Altar.*

Fifthly, All *Civill States* with their *Officers* of *justice* in their respective *constitutions* and *administrations* are proved *essentially Civill,* and therefore not *Judges, Governours* or *Defendours* of the *Spirituall* or *Christian state* and *Worship.*

Sixthly. It is the will and command of *God,* that (since the comming of his Sonne the Lord Jesus) a *permission* of the most *Paganish, Jewish, Turkish,* or *Antichristian consciences* and *worships,* bee granted to *all* men in all *Nations* and *Countries:* and they are onely to bee *fought* against with that *Sword* which is only (in *Soule matters*) *able* to *conquer,* to wit, the *Sword of Gods Spirit,* the *Word of God* . . . .

Eighthly, *God* requireth not an *uniformity* of *Religion* to be *inacted* and *inforced* in any *civill state;* which inforced *uniformity* (sooner or later) is the greatest occasion of *civill Warr,* ravishing of *conscience, persecution* of *Christ Jesus* in his servants, and of the *hypocrisie* and *destruction* of *millions of souls* . . . .

Tenthly, an inforced *uniformity* of *Religion* throughout a *Nation* or *civill state,* confounds the *Civill* and *Religious,* denies the principles of Christianity and civility, and that *Jesus Christ* is come in the Flesh.

Eleventhly, The permission of other *consciences* and *worships* than a state professeth, only can (according to God) procure a firme and lasting peace, (good *assurance* being taken according to the *wisdome* of the *civill state* for *uniformity* of *civill obedience* from all sorts.)

Twelfthly, lastly, true *civility* and *Christianity* may both flourish in a *state* or *Kingdome,* notwithstanding the permission of divers and contrary *consciences,* either *Jew* or *Gentile.*[5]

Needless to say, such "radical" views as these expressed by Roger Williams in 1644 did not immediately change the picture of the dominant outlook toward establishment, but they did take root increasingly and ever more firmly among larger numbers of people, especially among the non-conformist and dissenting groups that came to America in increasing numbers in the seventeenth and eighteenth centuries. Although the roots of establishment seemed firmly grounded in the soil of the seventeenth century, new seeds were soon planted that began rapidly to sprout and blossom into sturdy plants of religious freedom. Above all, the most important factor in the growth of freedom was the rapid increase of a wide variety of religious groups which soon began to attack the entrenched establishments where they existed and which effectively prevented the spread of establishment to ground where it had not originally been.

In general there were three types of attitudes toward religious establishments among the thirteen colonies. There was, first, the group of colonies where strong establishments existed for relatively long periods of time. These included Massachusetts, Connecticut, and New Hampshire, where the Congregational Church was most commonly recognized as the established church, and Virginia, South Carolina, and North Carolina, where the Church of England was established.

There was a second group of colonies in which little or no establishment ever existed and which were founded upon a large measure of religious freedom. These were Rhode Island, Pennsylvania, and Delaware.

There was, finally, a third group in which the status of establishment was uncertain or changed as the complexion of the religious population changed. These were New York, New Jersey, Maryland, and Georgia. In New York under the

Dutch rule the Dutch Reformed Church was established, but when the English came into power a long struggle ensued concerning the role of the Church of England in New York. The British crown, the royal governor, and the Anglican clergy assumed that the Church of England was established, but the colonial assembly, the Dutch Reformed Church, and the dissenters never admitted this claim. On the basis of actual practice for nearly a century it is clear that multiple rather than single establishment was the rule in New York (see pages 26-29 following).

The proprietors of New Jersey allowed a considerable amount of free exercise, of religion. When New Jersey was made into a royal province in 1702, the crown and royal governor again tried to assume that the Church of England was established, but the New Jersey legislature never passed such a law and never levied a tax for the support of religion. Thus the Church of England could not be considered as established in New Jersey. Maryland was founded under Lord Baltimore upon the basis of religious freedom, but when Maryland was made an English royal province in 1692, the Church of England was soon legally established by the colonial legislature. Georgia was also founded upon the basis of religious freedom; however, the Church of England was formally established after Georgia became a royal province in 1752, but it was not long in existence and never very effective in practice.

By the time of the Revolution, all colonies were trying in greater or lesser degree the experiment of allowing more freedom of religious worship. The American people were taking their first step in the direction of separation of church and state. Where establishments were strong, the first step was extremely difficult to take and many compromises were reached. These compromises often took the form of maintaining the establishment but granting toleration for dissenting sects to conduct religious exercises of their own. This was one phase of the third choice before the American people as described on page 8, namely, single establishment with some religious freedom. Sometimes the compromise took the form of expanding the establishment to grant privileges and tax support to more than one religious group while still maintaining some discrimination against other sects. This was the second phase of this same choice, namely, multiple establishment with some religious freedom. Only a few details and examples can be filled in here, but the trend is clear.

In the founding of Providence plantation, Roger Williams put into practice what he had preached. He sought to punish no one because of conscience and to exact obedience to the state only in civil matters. In the royal charter granted to Rhode Island in 1663, no one was to be asked to account for his religious beliefs so long as he did not disturb the civil peace. The British crown apparently felt that it would be good policy to encourage a colony that seemed likely to be advantageous for the Empire. If religious freedom contributed to prosperity, then religious freedom was to be encouraged. In general, Rhode Island was able to maintain its liberal record, although later, citizenship was limited to Protestant Christians, but this rule was not rigorously enforced, and some Jews and Catholics became citizens. There was no penal legislation against Quakers, Jews, or Catholics, and one of the strongest Jewish congregations grew up in Newport in the eighteenth century.

Maryland and Pennsylvania were both founded to provide havens for persecuted religious groups. The first Lord Baltimore hoped that Maryland would become such a refuge for Roman Catholics, but when they did not migrate in sufficient numbers the Act of Toleration of 1649 was passed to attract Protestants — who then came in such numbers that the Puritans among them were eventually able to pass laws discriminating against Catholics. Later, the Act of Toleration was again put in force, and, later still, the Church of England was established when Maryland became a royal province, but dissenters were tolerated (except Catholics). Despite the swing back and forth in control of the state, the heterogeneous population prevented the rigorous type of establishment found in New England or Virginia.

To William Penn the ideal of toleration and commercial interest were strong motives for founding Pennsylvania. Freedom of conscience and of worship was included in Penn's *Frame of Government* and was further re-enforced in the Great Law of 1682. The state was not to compel individuals to attend any public worship they did not wish to attend nor penalize them for their benefits. Society was to be founded upon Christian principles but without enforced conformity or uniformity. Freedom of conscience thus came to mean freedom from obligation to support anyone else's religion by taxation. The growth and prosperity of Pennsylvania stimulated other colonies to try more religious freedom. When Delaware was separated from Pennsylvania in 1702, Delaware continued the policy of permitting a wide range of religious freedom with no establishment of religion.

MULTIPLE ESTABLISHMENTS

Whereas some colonies moved toward religious freedom with no establishments, others tried to provide greater free exercise by granting financial, legal, and moral support by the state to several religious groups rather than to a single religious group. Multiple establishment thus became the policy for varying lengths of time in New York, Massachusetts, Connecticut, New Hampshire, Maryland, and South Carolina. It was attempted but not achieved in Virginia.

Under the Dutch commercial company which founded New Netherlands, the Dutch Reformed Church was established, but a distinction was made between public worship on one hand and private religious beliefs and private worship on the other. Even though public worship was confined to the Dutch

Reformed Church, considerable toleration was given to freedom of private conscience. This developed partly from indifference on the part of the governing company and partly from the desire to maintain a prosperous colony that would attract settlers. As a result, a heterogeneous religious population soon appeared, including Calvinists, Lutherans, Mennonites, Quakers, Catholics, and Jews. At first none of these groups were strong enough to achieve public worship for themselves, but soon the situation changed. When they did try to achieve public worship and when they met with strong measures of reprisal from Peter Stuyvesant, the Dutch West India Company supported them against Stuyvesant and greater tolerance was on the way.

When the English took over New Netherlands and made it into New York, the principle of toleration was continued. The inclinations of the Duke of York toward Catholicism led to a modification of the harsh measures against Catholics, and toleration for public worship was given to all Protestant groups who could produce an ordained minister. This principle of free exercise, as set down in the *Duke's Laws* of 1664, is interesting because no mention is made of the Church of England by name. The usual provisions for churches to be built and ministers to be supported by a public tax upon all inhabitants are included, but the Church of England was not singled out for special privilege. Each township was required to support a minister, but the minister was to be elected by the majority vote of the inhabitants of the town.

Thus, no specific church was to be established for the whole colony, but simply religion in general was to be established. Each town must have some kind of church and support it, but its denomination was to be left to the locality. Here is an early case where establishment did *not* mean preference of one religious group over all others; the preacher merely had to produce a certificate of ordination from some Protestant bishop or minister. The early English governors followed this practice of multiple establishment by recognizing that the Dutch Reformed Church be maintained as the established church and the Dutch minister be paid by public funds in certain towns.

After the Duke of York became king he then specifically instructed the royal governors to single out the Church of England for preference as the established church in New York and for public support of Anglican ministers. This set off a long period of conflict with the New York Assembly which consistently refused to pass such laws. Upon the insistence of the royal governor, Benjamin Fletcher, the New York Assembly finally passed a compromise law in 1693 which carefully refrained from giving preference to the Church of England. The act simply provided that in six towns of the four southern counties of New York there should be "established a good, sufficient, Protestant Minister" to be supported by a public tax. This act did not mention the Church of England, it applied only to New York City, Richmond, Westchester, and Queens, it made no mention of the denomination of the ministers to be chosen, and it did not apply to the whole province.[6]

From then on the battle raged between the royal governors and the Anglican clergymen on one side, who maintained that the Church of England was established, and the legislature and the dissenters on the other side who insisted that it was not. In 1695 the Assembly specifically resolved that a town in the four counties specified could select a dissenting Protestant minister and pay him from public tax funds. Controversy ensued in many disputes and court cases. One of the most notable cases was decided in 1731 when a court ruled that the town of Jamaica in Queens could select and support a Presbyterian minister rather than a Church of England minister as the established minister of the town. Here was the principle of "co-operation" between the state and a variety of churches. This policy of multiple establishment was maintained in New York until the time of the Revolution when it was abrogated in the New York Constitution of 1777. Even the wording of the New York Constitution reveals the determination not to admit that the Church of England had been a single establishment. Article XXXV reads:

> That all such parts of the said common law, and all such of the said statutes and acts aforesaid, or parts thereof, *as may be construed to establish or maintain any particular denomination of Christians or their ministers,* . . . be, and they hereby are, abrogated and rejected.[7]

The trend toward multiple establishment was even more clearly evident in Massachusetts, Connecticut, and New Hampshire, but it has not been so easily recognized because of the firm place the dominant Congregational majority held in the political and religious affairs of the New England colonies. Because the Congregational Puritan churches were so commonly the established churches in New England, it is often forgotten that *legally* it was possible for a large number of religious groups to participate in the establishment by the time the First Amendment was being formulated in 1789.

In Massachusetts the single establishment of the Congregational Church received a body blow when William and Mary issued the new charter of 1691, making Massachusetts a royal province, granting toleration to all Protestants, and removing membership in the Congregational Church as a prerequisite for the suffrage. Thus, the groundwork was laid for the growth of other religious groups which were to challenge the dominance of the single establishment. These were principally Anglicans, Baptists, and Quakers. The Congregationalist majority in the General Court, however, circumvented the edict of toleration by promptly passing a law in 1692 which compelled each *town* to support and maintain "an able, orthodox and learned minister" by means of a religious tax upon all inhabitants.[8] Although the Congregational Church was thus not singled out by name for preference in tax support, the Congregationalists had a sufficient majority in the towns to make sure that the voters would for a long time choose a Congregationalist minister to be the established minister. From then on it was a battle between the Congregationalist majority who tried to use the civil machinery of the state to protect their privileges and the dissenters who, on their part, tried to gain privileges or exemptions for themselves.

The first groups to be successful in this effort were Church of England members who were given the privilege in a law of 1727 to have their religious taxes paid to their own ministers for their support. Here was recognition of the principle of multiple establishment. There was no longer a single establishment when the civil taxing authorities were used to aid the Episcopalians to support their churches along with the Congregational churches. Then, in the following years the Quakers and Baptists were granted exemption by law from paying taxes for the Congregational town churches if they could obtain certificates showing that they were regular attending members of their own services. All others were required to pay taxes for the support of the town churches.

The dissenters kept up a constant running fight against the principle of establishment, especially after the Revolutionary period, but they lost their fight in the Massachusetts Constitution of 1780 which gave the legislature authority to compel the towns to levy a general tax to support "public Protestant teachers of piety, religion, and morality" to be chosen by the "several towns, parishes, precincts, and other bodies politic, or religious societies." The constitution of 1780 and the laws soon passed under it were a step backward for the Quakers and Baptists who now were not exempt from religious taxes, but had to pay the taxes and then obtain a certificate which entitled *their own* ministers or religious teachers to obtain their share of the taxes from the taxing authorities.

Article III of the Massachusetts Constitution of 1780 contains the following provision:

And all moneys paid by the subject to the support of public worship, and of the public teachers aforesaid, shall, if he require it, be uniformly applied to the support of the public teacher or teachers of his own religious sect or denomination, provided there be any on whose instruction he attends; otherwise it may be paid towards the support of the teacher or teachers of the parish or precinct in which the said moneys are raised.[9]

Here was a thoroughgoing multiple establishment in which everyone still paid a general tax for religion, but the way had been opened for all Protestant groups to participate equally in the privileges of the establishment. Any group could set itself up as a parish or precinct and claim its share of religious taxes. A court decided that even so radical a dissenter as a Universalist minister in Gloucester was entitled to recover the taxes that his parishioners had paid to the town treasury. The town form of multiple establishment was the constitutional policy of Massachusetts in 1789 when the First Amendment was framed and continued to be until an amendment to the Massachusetts Constitution was adopted in 1833. New Hampshire followed in main respects the Massachusetts town form of multiple establishment from its law of 1714, down to and including its constitution of 1784.

The story of multiple establishment in Connecticut was similar. Connecticut named the Congregational Church as the establishment when the General Court approved the Saybrook Platform in 1708 and then moved to the town form of multiple establishment by a law of 1717 which provided for the election of the town minister by a majority of the voters and empowered the town to levy taxes for his support. (*Connecticut Records*, IV, 33.) Connecticut also passed a law in 1727 giving Church of England members the right to use their taxes for the support of their own ministers and even to levy further taxes if the original taxes were not deemed sufficient.[10] Quakers and Baptists were also given exemption from paying taxes for the town establishments.

In 1784 in its first code of laws as a state Connecticut authorized each town to form one or more ecclesiastical societies as the majority of inhabitants so voted in order to levy taxes for the support of public ministers. It also authorized dissenters to form their own societies which were to be on an equal footing with the same privileges of supporting their ministers by taxation as those of the majority churches.[11] Everyone had to support some kind of religious worship, but he could choose which kind. This was the general form of multiple establishment which obtained in Connecticut from 1784 until the dissenting groups became strong enough to oust the Congregationalists from political power and adopt the Connecticut Constitution of 1818 which finally wiped out the town form of multiple establishment and made religious support a purely voluntary matter. The state could no longer use its civil machinery to support or promote one or more forms of religion.

In Virginia the established Church of England began to feel the pressures for toleration as early as 1685 when the home government issued instructions to the governor in Virginia to allow freedom of conscience to all persons who did not threaten the civil peace, although this was amended in 1690 to exclude Catholics from toleration. By 1699 the principles of the English *Act of Toleration* of 1689 were in effect, namely, that all dissenter groups whose ministers and places of worship were registered could hold public worship. Thus, Presbyterians and Baptists began to settle in the western regions of Virginia. When they began to move into the eastern sections, however, they began to suffer retaliation. The presence of dissenters in growing numbers laid the conditions which led to demands for multiple establishment. It was this effort to achieve multiple establishment which was blocked by the leadership of Madison and Jefferson soon after the Revolution (see Chapter 3). ⊬

The efforts of the older establishments to arrive at multiple establishment were crowned, however, with greater success in Maryland and South Carolina than they were in Virginia. At the beginning of the Revolution, strong Church of England groups were able to hold off complete disestablishment for a while by inserting provisions for multiple establishment in the constitutions of Maryland and South Carolina. In both states the constitutional provisions tried to reach a compromise whereby free exercise of religion would be protected on one hand, while at the same time provision was made for multiple establishment and protection for the property of the Church of England.

A close reading of the Maryland Constitution of 1776 will reveal how the attempt was made to serve all of these varying interests at the same time. First, respects were paid to free exercise of religion; then, secondly, multiple establishment was made legal; and, finally, the property of the Church of England was safeguarded:

That, as it is the duty of every man to worship God in such manner as he thinks most acceptable to him; all persons, professing the Christian religion, are equally entitled to protection in their religious liberty; wherefore no person ought by any law to be molested in his person or estate on account of his religious persuasion or profession, or for his religious practice; unless, under colour of religion, any man shall disturb the good order, peace or safety of the State, or shall infringe the laws of morality, or injure others, in their natural, civil, or religious rights; *nor ought any person to be compelled to frequent or maintain, or contribute, unless on contract, to maintain any particular place of worship, or any particular ministry; yet the Legislature may, in their discretion, lay a general and equal tax, for the support of the Christian religion: leaving to each individual the power of appointing the payment over of the money, collected from him, to the support of any particular place of worship or minister,* or for the benefit of the poor of his own denomination, or the poor in general of any particular county: but the churches, chapels, glebes, and all other property now belonging to the Church of England, ought to remain to the Church of England forever.[12]

A careful reading of these provisions will show that the meaning of establishment had definitely moved away from support of a single preferred church to support for any Christian sect so designated by the taxpayer. All Christian churches were on an equal footing in the eyes of the law. This was multiple establishment. The people of Maryland recognized it as multiple establishment when they ratified a constitutional amendment in 1810 specifically outlawing this provision in the following words:

Art. XIII. That it shall not be lawful for the general assembly of this State to lay an equal and general tax, or any other tax, on the people of this State, for the support of *any religion.*[13]

Similar, but much more elaborate, provisions for multiple establishment were included in the South Carolina Constitution of 1778. These provisions illustrate so clearly the common and widespread understanding that establishment of religion meant multiple establishment that they deserve to be quoted at length:

That all persons and religious societies who acknowledge that there is one God, and a future state of rewards and punishments, and that God is publicly to be worshipped, shall be freely tolerated. *The Christian Protestant religion shall be deemed, and is hereby constituted and declared to be, the established religion of this State. That all denominations of Christian Protestants in this State, demeaning themselves peaceably and faithfully, shall enjoy equal religious and civil privileges.* To accomplish this desirable purpose without injury to the religious property of those societies of Christians which are by law already incorporated for the purpose of religious worship, and *to put it fully into the power of every other society of Christian Protestants, either already formed or hereafter to be formed, to obtain the like incorporation,* it is hereby constituted, appointed, and declared that the respective societies of the Church of England that are already formed in this State for the purpose of religious worship shall continue incorporate and hold the religious property now in their possession. And that whenever fifteen or more male persons, not under twenty-one years of age, professing the Christian Protestant religion, and agreeing to unite themselves in a society for the purposes of religious worship, they shall, (on complying with the terms hereinafter mentioned), be, and be constituted a church, and *be ESTEEMED AND REGARDED in law as of the established religion of the State,* and on a petition to the legislature shall be *entitled* to be incorporated and *to enjoy equal privileges.* That every society of Christians so formed shall give themselves a name or denomination by which they shall be called and known in law, and all that associate with them for the purposes of worship shall be esteemed as belonging to the society so called. But that previous to *the establishment and incorporation of the respective societies of every denomination* as aforesaid, and in order to entitle them thereto, each society so petitioning shall have agreed to and subscribed in a book the following five articles, without which no agreement or union of men upon *pretence of religion* shall entitle them to be incorporated and *esteemed as a church of the established religion of this state:*

1st. That there is one eternal God, and a future state of rewards and punishments.
2d. That God is publicly to be worshipped.
3d. That the Christian religion is the true religion.
4th. That the holy scriptures of the Old and New Testaments are of divine inspiration, and are the rule of faith and practice.
5th. That it is lawful and the duty of every man being thereunto called by those that govern, to bear witness to the truth.[14]

It is true, of course, that the Constitution of South Carolina still discriminated against Roman Catholics and non-Christians, but no one can read these words carefully and still maintain that establishment meant simply a privilege for a single religious sect or denomination in preference to all others.

All Protestant Christian sects were to be treated equally and impartially by the state. This was a great broadening of the meaning of establishment from the days when the Church of England was actually a single establishment and civil disabilities were laid upon Puritans, Presbyterians, Baptists, Quakers, and all other dissenting Protestant sects as well as upon Roman Catholics and non-Christians. All significant religious groups in South Carolina could thus participate equally in the multiple establishment. It was but an easy step to open the establishment to all Christians and include Catholics. This was done in Maryland where Catholics represented a major group, and it was attempted in Virginia in the years between 1779 and 1786.

The next and final step in the expansion of the meaning of establishment would be simply to say that *all* religious groups should be given support by the state. This step was almost achieved in the assessment bill in Virginia in 1784 (see page 59). This is the step which some religious groups today are urging as the proper relationship of "co-operation" between church and state. But the people of the late eighteenth and nineteenth centuries refused to take this step. They even refused to accept for long the principle of multiple establishment. They were no better satisfied with multiple establishment than they were with single establishment. They found that both forms of establishment were blocks on the road to genuine freedom of religion.

In summary, then, just prior to the Revolution the principle of toleration of dissenting religious beliefs had gained considerable headway. It might even be said that the principle of free exercise of religion had become a powerful force in the American scene. The "Great Awakening" of the middle of the eighteenth century with its stimulus to evangelical religions and its enormous impetus to the growth of the "popular" churches had stimulated the expansion of Congregational, Baptist, Presbyterian, Methodist, and other denominations.

Strong elements within each of these groups were opposed to establishment, were struggling for freedom, and were ready from this point of view to support that phase of the eighteenth century Enlightenment which began to preach that freedom of religious conscience was a natural right of all men.

When the doctrine of natural rights was applied to religion and was expressed in the form of "equal rights of conscience," the majority of Americans eventually came to see that equal rights of conscience meant more than mere toleration of dissenting beliefs. It was realized that, whereas toleration and free exercise of religion might exist alongside establishment, *equal* rights of conscience could *not* be achieved while establishment in either its single of multiple form existed. So long as the state had any remaining right to sit in judgment upon the claims of *any* religious faith or to tax persons for the support of any religious teaching in which they did not believe, there could be no equal rights of conscience. Until *all* religious claims were considered equal in the eyes of the state, the smallest group equally with the largest, the "insignificant" equally with the influential, the "offensive" equally with the orthodox, establishment stood in the way of equal rights of conscience. When Americans recognized that all forms of establishment were hostile to equality, they formulated the conception of separation of church and state in the Revolutionary and early National period. They then chose the fourth alternative as described on page 9.

The principle of separation of church and state, as will appear in Chapter 3, was one of the achievements necessary for the creation of the new society that was in process of formation with the opening of the Revolutionary period. So long as men believed that morality rested upon specific religious beliefs, the state could not tolerate dissenters, for dissenting religious belief would imply immoral conduct inimical to the common welfare of civil society. When men began to grant that a person could be morally good and thus could be a good citizen even though he did not accept the dominant religious doctrines, the idea of establishment was threatened and separation was indicated.

More and more people came to believe, as Chapter 3 will show, that freedom of religion required the assumption that there are different religious roads to the good life and that *genuine* religious freedom required that the state guarantee equal rights of conscience to all religious claimants with no distinctions. They argued that a thorough acceptance of the equal rights of conscience required that morality could not be confined to those expressing some recognized religious or church doctrine.

The next step was to grant that in a democratic society the non-believer as well as the believer in some one of several recognized religious doctrines must be accorded the right to be considered capable of good moral conduct and of good citizenship. The test of good citizenship is morality, not religious belief. Thus when the colonists decided to renounce their connection with Britain and become Americans, they also decided that their differing religious beliefs could not be allowed to stand in the way of the common ties of good citizenship. They therefore moved to separate the state from all churches as well as from any one church, so that all Americans could become equally good citizens in the eyes of the civil law and of the state. The recognition that, so far as the state is concerned, good citizenship rests upon good conduct and not upon religious belief was the secular revolution that accompanied the political revolution. This recognition took the institutional form of separation of church and state.

3

The Principle of Separation in the Original States

THE HISTORICAL MEANING of separation of church and state cannot be determined by a narrow analysis of any specific event in any one place at any one time. It must be seen as a developing principle and practice that had its roots in the past and that took form on an uneven front throughout the new nation that was struggling to come into existence during the Revolutionary and early National periods. It was a principle that emerged more rapidly in some states and more slowly in others. But the trend was unmistakable.

In some states where establishment had never gained a foothold and the practice of religious freedom was strong, there was little or no problem of separation as in Rhode Island, Pennsylvania, and Delaware. In other states where the establishment was strong, where the religious population was highly homogeneous, and where the tradition of religious freedom was weak, the principle of separation was slower in formulation and in practice, as in Massachusetts, Connecticut, and New Hampshire. In still other states where the establishment was strong but where the religious population was rapidly becoming heterogeneous, the process of separation and the formulation of the principle of separation was relatively rapid, notably in Virginia. Thus it took Virginia scarcely ten years from 1776 to 1786 to complete the process by legal enactment, whereas it took Massachusetts more than fifty years from 1776 to 1833 to arrive at virtually the same stage in its constitutional development.

It was in the midst of this unmistakable historical process that the First Amendment was debated in Congress in 1789 and finally ratified in 1791. The meaning of the First Amendment *cannot* be discovered by a narrow examination of the meaning of its specific words at a specific time, but those words must receive their meaning from the more inclusive process in which they were formulated, debated, and approved. Any sound historical interpretation of the meaning of the First Amendment should be derived from the larger cultural setting in which it was developed. No narrow historicism will suffice. The indisputable fact, as we shall see in the next few pages, is that the American people were moving from establishment to separation in the Revolutionary and early National periods; they were moving in different states at different rates and it is fair to say from different motives, but they were moving.

The First Amendment was an integral part of this movement. It was sponsored by and fought for by persons who had been through the process in their own states or who otherwise clearly saw the direction of the trend as did the followers of the Enlightenment. The framers of the First Amendment were in the vanguard of the movement. The First Amendment thus reflected the most advanced thinking on the subject of separation at the time of its adoption, and it in turn not only showed the way but speeded up the process in the laggard states.

In general, the process of separation, from the pre-Revolutionary to the early National periods, went through three identifiable stages:

(1) *Toleration by the single establishments*

Dissenting groups and the leaders who believed in

religious freedom continued and speeded up the fight against the established churches in the effort to win the right to the free exercise of public religious worship. This right they wrung from the conservative groups in state after state in the form of concessions and the granting of privileges of free worship. Something of this process has been described in Chapter 2.

(2) *Multiple establishments*

The liberal groups believing in religious freedom discovered, however, that they were still in an underprivileged position because the legal support of taxes and property rights was still assigned by the state to the established churches. They discovered that "free exercise" was still a shadowy grant of toleration so long as the established churches had the support of tithes and so they renewed the fight to disestablish more completely the favored churches. The established churches, on their part, tried to compromise by persuading the legislatures to open up the tax privileges to the dissenting groups one by one. This meant that gradually more and more churches were admitted into the establishment and given the legal rights of taxation for their own public worship.

Thus, "establishment" came to be applied, not just to *one* church, but to any or all churches that had legal and financial connections with the state. This extended meaning of "establishment" was widely recognized at the time of the passing of the First Amendment. *Any* co-operation between the state and any or all churches was considered to be "establishment." In some states this compromise was agreed upon and was maintained for a relatively long time, as in Massachusetts, Connecticut, and New Hampshire; in other states the compromise lasted for only a short time, as in Maryland and South Carolina. In still other states the effort to achieve this compromise was defeated, notably in Virginia. It was this expanded meaning of multiple establishment that the First Amendment was designed to prevent on the national level as well as to prevent the narrow establishment of a single church.

At the time of the formulation and ratification of the First Amendment in the period 1789-1791 all states that still had some form of establishment in effect had moved into the form of multiple establishment. As described in Chapter 2, Massachusetts, Connecticut, and New Hampshire all provided for their distinctive town form of multiple establishment, and Maryland and South Carolina had provided for their respective state forms of multiple establishment. These were the only states in which establishment was still recognized in the basic laws of the several states, when the debates over the First Amendment began in 1789. South Carolina quickly dropped its elaborate provisions for multiple establishment from its constitution of 1790, whereas Maryland did not amend its constitution until 1810.

Thus, in 1789 five of the original states still had authorized establishments. They were all multiple establishments. Before the First Amendment was ratified in 1791, South Carolina had eliminated its constitutional provisions for multiple establishment. After the adoption of the First Amendment in 1791 there were only four states whose basic laws embodied the principle of establishment. The Massachusetts Constitution of 1780 and the Connecticut codified laws of 1784 made multiple establishment compulsory; Maryland's Constitution of 1776 and New Hampshire's Constitutions of 1784 and 1791 *permitted* multiple establishments at the discretion of the legislatures.

It is this meaning of multiple establishment which has been forgotten, conveniently overlooked, or never understood by the various groups today who urge that "co-operation" between church and state is admissible so long as the state treats all religious groups equally and fairly. *That was exactly the purpose* of the several colonial provisions for multiple establishment as described in Chapter 2, and it was exactly the purpose of the attempts made in Virginia to achieve multiple establishment, as will be described in the following pages. Of course, they would have ruled out some sects which the dominant churches did not consider to be "safe" or legitimate religious groups, but the principle of multiple establishment is the same whether few, many, or all religious groups are taken into it. The state would always have to decide what was and what was not a religious group if it set out to "co-operate" with them all.

(3) *Separation*

It was soon discovered that the compromise of establishing all recognized churches even on an equal or impartial basis was not sufficient. It might be possible to reconcile this kind of establishment with the outward forms of free exercise of public worship, but it was soon clearly seen that it could not be reconciled with genuinely *equal* rights of conscience. So long as the state was in the position of determining which churches should have legal and financial privileges of support, there could be no real equality of religious conscience. It was still a grant of privilege by the state to a religious doctrine. Such a principle could not square with the growing belief fostered by the Enlightenment that equal rights of conscience were natural and inalienable rights which the state could not infringe and which the state must protect.

Therefore, the struggle went on to sever all legal connections and to prohibit all financial support for any and all religious beliefs. It was recognized that if the state could grant a privilege, it could define which religious beliefs were entitled to that privilege. So the final stage in separation came when all forms of establishment were abolished. Thus, complete disestablishment of financial and legal support for religion by the state was necessary to achieve a genuinely free exercise of religion resting upon the solid grounds of equal rights of conscience.

This final step was clearly in the minds of those who proposed and struggled for the adoption of the First Amendment of the Constitution. The First Amendment was clearly an integral part of the larger definition of civil rights as contained in the other amendments which made up the American Bill of Rights.

The whole story of this historical process in the course of which the principle of separation of church and state emerged should be told in detail state by state, but the necessities of space limit us to presenting only one example of a state which had a strong establishment. This example, Virginia, shows the completion of the process *before* the First Amendment was formulated, and is important because the leaders in Congress from Virginia were the ones who gave the primary form to the First Amendment as it went through the various stages of debate and adoption.

Other examples among the original states could be given to show that the process of separation was well under way in a majority of states *before* the adoption of the First Amendment. Separation had already been achieved in eight of the original states. This was accomplished in the constitutions of 1776 of New Jersey, Pennsylvania, Delaware, and North Carolina; in the constitutions of 1777 of New York and Georgia; by statute of 1786 in Virginia; and by original charter in Rhode Island.

The fact that some states did not complete the process of separation until after the First Amendment simply means that they were somewhat later in a process of which the First Amendment was at once a reflection and also a formative influence. The First Amendment was the application on the national level of the same principle that was developing in the states.

THE STRUGGLE FOR SEPARATION IN VIRGINIA

The struggle for separation of church and state in Virginia highlighted the movement in other sections of the country where the Church of England was established. Separation of church and state was a part of the larger revolutionary struggle for separation from England; the Church of England was closely identified with the crown in the minds of Americans. Thus, religious liberty and civil liberty were often closely associated. Just prior to the Revolution, the Anglican groups tried to establish an American bishop to be in charge of all Anglican churches in America rather than to maintain the Anglican church as subordinate to the Bishop of London. This move intensified the fears of dissenters that they would lose even what liberties they had gained. Also the Quebec Act of 1774 which gave privileges of tax support to the Roman Catholic Church in Canada intensified fears of Protestants in America that the English government was not to be trusted to preserve religious freedom.

On the home front, the separation of church and state was a part of the larger revolutionary struggle to replace an aristocratic social, political, and economic system with a more democratic and "republican" system. Thus, in general, the "liberal" groups politically were in favor of separation and the "conservative" groups politically were defenders of establishment. Insofar as the English political labels applied to America, Whigs were for separation and Tories were for establishment. When party lines were drawn during the early years of the new nation, Federalists tended to favor establishment and Democratic-Republicans tended to favor separation. These are broad generalizations subject to qualification, but, taking the country as a whole, the religious establishments were viewed along with other political, economic, and social privileges of the old order as objects for change in the effort to create a more equalitarian and democratic society along the lines of the natural rights doctrines of the Declaration of Independence. In its broader setting, then, the struggle for separation of church and state was an integral part of the Revolutionary struggle "for home rule" and the struggle to see "who would rule at home."

These lines between conservatives and liberals were clearly apparent in the Virginia Convention of 1776 which set up a committee to draft a Declaration of Rights and a constitution for Virginia. It was on this committee that the young James Madison began his long and notable fight for separation of church and state as one of the cornerstones of the new nation which was about to be created. The first draft of the Declaration of Rights of the Virginia Constitution is attributed to George Mason whose article on religion included the clause:

> . . . religion . . . can be governed only by reason and conviction, not by force or violence; and therefore all men should enjoy the fullest toleration in the exercise of religion, according to the dictates of conscience, unpunished and unrestrained by the magistrates. . . .[1]

This emphasis upon toleration was obviously the reflection of an outlook that held that the established church should be maintained but that "free exercise" of public worship for dissenters should be granted at the discretion of the state.

Realizing that the principle of toleration was not enough to achieve complete religious freedom, Madison proposed a substitute for the article on religion which went much further toward complete separation. Madison's proposal read in part:

> . . . Religion . . . being under the direction of reason and conviction only, not of violence or compulsion, all men are equally entitled to the full and free exercise of it, according to the dictates of conscience; and therefore . . . no man or class of men ought, on account of religion, to be invested with peculiar emoluments or privileges, nor subjected to any penalties or disabilities . . . .[2]

By striking out "toleration" and emphasizing *equality* of the *rights* of conscience as the basis for free exercise, Madison was expressing a much more thoroughgoing principle, a principle of religious freedom that went far beyond John Locke's conception of religious toleration and expressed the doctrines of natural rights upon which so much of the theoretical basis of the Revolution was based. By striking out "force" and substituting "compulsion" Madison would have deprived the state of legal and financial power to support religion or to control religious beliefs in any way. Madison's emphasis upon denying "peculiar emoluments or privileges" to any clergy or church members also looked toward disestablishment of financial or legal support of religion by the state. The principle of separation was clearly envisioned by Madison's substitute proposal. He was thinking in terms of eighteenth century natural rights rather than in terms of seventeenth century toleration.

It was soon apparent, however, that Madison could not achieve such a radical separation at once, for his proposal was not accepted in full, but after more committee work he was able to insert the first part of his proposal concerning the equal rights of conscience. His emphasis upon compulsion and his clause concerning disestablishment, however, were not accepted, and the final version of the article on religion in the Virginia Declaration of Rights of 1776 as modified by Madison and as approved by the Convention was as follows:

That religion, or the duty which we owe to our Creator, and the manner of discharging it, can be directed only by reason and conviction, not by force or violence; and therefore all men are equally entitled to the free exercise of religion, according to the dictates of conscience; and that it is the mutual duty of all to practise Christian forbearance, love, and charity towards each other.[3]

Although Madison was active on the ground in the Virginia Convention, it is important to note Jefferson's attitude toward the religious issue during the times when he was absent from Virginia on other business. During the framing of the Virginia Constitution, Jefferson was in Philadelphia as Virginia delegate to the Continental Congress where, among other duties, he framed the Declaration of Independence. Despite his preoccupation in Congress Jefferson found time in June 1776 to write a comprehensive proposed draft for a Virginia Constitution, but his draft did not reach Williamsburg in time to be considered by the Virginia Convention. Therefore, the Convention used Mason's more conservative draft as a working document instead of Jefferson's more liberal proposals.

Jefferson's attitude toward disestablishment is clearly revealed in his proposed draft for the Virginia Constitution which included, under the section on "Rights, Private and Public," the following provision:

> All persons shall have full and free liberty of religious opinion; nor shall any be compelled to frequent or *maintain any religious institution.*[4]

Here, in Jefferson's clear-cut language, is his definitive statement of his outlook in 1776 on the relation between church and state. The first clause of his provision deals with guaranteeing free exercise of religion; the second clause deals with prohibiting compulsory support for *any religious institution.* These latter words (which became the basis for his Bill for Religious Freedom introduced in 1779 and passed in 1786) demonstrate as clearly as any words could do that Jefferson was opposed to multiple establishment. These words need merely be compared with Mason's proposals for "toleration" to see that Jefferson would have outlawed state support for *all* religious institutions just as much as he would have outlawed support for the single Church of England. To try to claim that Jefferson simply was opposed to single establishment is to ignore or overlook Jefferson's consistent opposition to all forms of establishment, single and multiple, an opposition which began as early as 1776 and continued without deviation to his death.

In describing Jefferson's role in Virginia, the most authoritative biographer of Jefferson has this to say:

> . . . in 1776 he probably was the foremost advocate of the entire separation of Church and State in Virginia, and unquestionably he became the major symbol of complete religious liberty in connection with his own measure. Such, he remained during the years that he played on a larger stage.[5]

To return to Madison, who reflected Jefferson's outlook, it is clear from the beginning that Madison saw that "free exercise" of religion based on toleration did *not* require disestablishment, but that "free exercise" based upon *equality* of conscience as a natural right *did* require disestablishment. From the beginning, these two elements in Madison's thinking paralleled those of Jefferson. Equality of conscience and disestablishment made up his conception of the principle of separation of church and state. He never swerved from that principle, and it was paramount in his mind when he took part in framing the First Amendment. Despite his failure to gain acceptance for the specific words that applied to the principle of disestablishment in the Virginia Declaration of Rights, the acceptance of Madison's words that embodied the principle of equal rights of conscience was a victory of the greatest proportions, for he looked upon the two as simply reverse sides of the same shield. His efforts during the next eleven years for the passage of laws in the Virginia Assembly which would write into the statutes the specific principle of disestablishment are proof of his loyalty to the full principle of separation. This loyalty was embodied in his activities in the first Congress which adopted the First Amendment in 1789 and in his outlook as President of the United States from 1808 to 1816.

The next step in the separation of church and state in Virginia was the passage of an act by the legislature in 1776 which began the statutory disestablishment of the Anglican Church. The committee on religion which was instructed to draw up the bill was composed not only of Madison and Mason but also of Thomas Jefferson who had by that time returned from Philadelphia where the Declaration of Independence had been signed a few months earlier. This bill which was passed on December 9, 1776 was essentially a compromise, for the conservative forces in the legislature were still strong, but it began the process of separation which was to be virtually completed within ten years.

The Act of 1776 achieved the following steps toward separation: (1) it repealed all acts that used the penal law of the state to prescribe religious beliefs, enforce church attendance, or enforce certain methods of worship, (2) it exempted all dissenters from the payment of taxes or levies to support the Anglican Church, and (3) beginning on January 1, 1777 it suspended until the next session of the Assembly (summer 1777) all taxes upon members of the Church of England for the support of Anglican clergymen.[6] Thus, dissenters were exempt entirely from religious taxes and members of the established church did not have to pay the taxes for their own clergy during the period of suspension. In effect, the financial prop for maintaining the established church by taxes was destroyed. The Assembly continued the suspension of taxes for Church of England members in successive sessions in 1777 and 1778, and finally passed an act of 1779 which repealed the earlier Act of 1748 which had originally made such levies legal. Thus the suspension was made permanent.

The Act of 1776 left three other matters unsolved: (1) It authorized the Church of England vestries to continue their authority to tax the local parishes for poor relief. (2) It reserved the glebe lands, church buildings, and church property for the use of the Anglican church and clergy. (3) It specifically stated that the question of levying a general assessment for *all* churches would be postponed. This latter was one of the most important struggles of all, for it would have broadened the meaning of establishment from simple to multiple establishment. It posed the question, in effect, "Shall the state require all persons to support the church of their choice, or shall support of churches be an exclusively voluntary affair?"

The solution of these three problems was required before separation could be complete, but the struggle over a general assessment was the critical struggle, for that was the decision to sever co-operative connection between the state and *all* churches. From 1776 to 1786 everyone in Virginia knew that the basic issue was the question of multiple establishment through general assessment, whereas the decision concerning vestries and the Anglican church property was simply the relatively minor decision to sever the remaining co-operative connections between the state and a single church. Here, as in all other states where establishments still existed, the principle of "free exercise" had been formally won; the only struggles remaining to be fought were over the question of financial support of religion at state expense.

The year 1779 was a critical year for these decisions in Virginia. The political liberals combined behind Jefferson's proposals to try to solve the religious problems on a broad base. They introduced a comprehensive set of bills designed to do away with the economic privileges of the landed aristocracy, to establish a state system of public schools, and to separate the church and state by means of Jefferson's Bill for Religious Freedom. These proposals showed clearly how the Jeffersonian democrats and liberals conceived the total problem of achieving a new kind of society based upon freedom, equality, and democracy. If they had all passed, there would have been no question about the early achievement of a public school system based upon secular, democratic rather than upon religious foundations. However, the conservatives defeated the public school proposals; the democrats won the economic proposals; and the religious question reached a stalemate for the moment.

Jefferson's Bill for Religious Freedom was a thoroughgoing statement of the principle of separation of church and state and revealed clearly what the democrats were struggling for. It was framed to combat the idea of general assessment and thus was intended to prevent multiple establishment as well as single establishment. In these memorable words, Jefferson stated the case for complete separation of church and state:

I.   Whereas Almighty God hath created the mind free . . . *to compel a man to furnish contributions of money for the propagation of opinions which he disbelieves, is sinful and tyrannical; that even the forcing him to support this or that teacher of his own religious persuasion, is depriving him of the comfortable liberty of giving his contributions to the particular pastor, whose morals he would make his pattern,* and whose powers he feels most persuasive to righteousness . . . therefore the proscribing any citizen as unworthy the public confidence by laying upon him an incapacity of being called to offices of trust and emolument, unless he profess or renounce this or that religious opinion, is depriving him injuriously of those privileges and advantages to which in common with his fellow citizens he has a natural right; that it tends only to corrupt the principles of that religion it is meant to encourage, by bribing with a monopoly of worldly honours and emoluments, those who will externally profess and conform to it . . . to suffer the civil magistrate to intrude his powers into the field of opinion, and to restrain the profession or propagation of principles on supposition of their ill tendency, is a dangerous fallacy, which at once destroys all religious liberty, because he being of course judge of that tendency will make his opinions the rule of judgment, and approve or condemn the sentiments of others only as they shall square with or differ from his own; that it is time enough for the rightful purposes of civil government, for its officers to interfere when principles break out into overt acts against peace and good order; and finally, that truth is great and will prevail if left to herself, that she is the proper and sufficient antagonist to error, and has nothing to fear from the conflict, unless by human interposition disarmed of her natural weapons, free argument and debate, errors ceasing to be dangerous when it is permitted freely to contradict them:

II.   *Be it enacted by the General Assembly,* That *no man shall be compelled to frequent or support any religious worship, place, or ministry whatsoever,* nor shall be enforced, restrained, molested, or burthened in his body or goods, nor shall otherwise suffer on account of his religious opinions or belief; but that all men shall be free to profess, and by argument to maintain, their opinion in matters of religion, and that the same shall in no wise diminish, enlarge, or affect their civil capacities.

III.   . . . the rights hereby asserted are of the natural rights of mankind, and that if any act shall be hereafter passed to repeal the present, or to narrow its operation, such act will be an infringement of natural right.[7]

The conservatives, on the other hand, met Jefferson's proposals with a bill of their own, introduced by James Henry, which is one of the clearest statements ever made of what "establishment" meant in 1779 to both conservatives and liberals.[8] Fearing that they were losing the battle to maintain a single established church, the conservatives now proposed that the state constitute *the Christian religion in general* as the established religion of the state and support *equally and impartially* all duly constituted Christian denominations by a general assessment levied upon all persons. This bill states so clearly the doctrine of multiple establishment in the name of free exercise of religion that it will be quoted at length.[9]

For the encouragement of Religion and virtue, and for removing all restraints on the mind in its inquiries after truth, Be it enacted by the General Assembly, that all persons and Religious Societies who acknowledge that there is one God, and a future State of rewards and punishments, and that God ought to be publickly worshiped, shall be freely tolerated.

The Christian Religion shall in all times coming be deemed and held to be the established Religion of this Commonwealth; and all Denominations of Christians demeaning themselves peaceably and faithfully, shall enjoy equal privileges, civil and Religious.

To accomplish this desirable purpose without injury to the property of those Societies of Christians already incorporated by Law for the purpose of Religious Worship, and to put it fully into the power of every other Society of Christians, either already formed or to be hereafter formed to obtain the like incorporation, Be it further enacted, that the respective Societies of the Church of England already formed in this Commonwealth, shall be continued Corporate, and hold the Religious property now in their possession for ever.

Whenever . . . free male Persons not under twenty one Years of age, professing the Christian Religion, shall agree to unite themselves in a Society for the purpose of Religious Worship, they shall be constituted a Church, and *esteemed and regarded in Law as of the established Religion of this Commonwealth,* and on their petition to the General Assembly shall be entitled to be incorporated and *shall enjoy equal Privileges with any other Society of Christians,* and all that associate with them for the purpose of Religious Worship, shall be esteemed as belonging to the Society so called.

Every Society so formed shall give themselves a name or denomination by which they shall be called and known in Law. And it is further enacted, that previous to the establishment and incorporation of the respective Societies of every denomination as aforesaid, and in order to entitle them thereto, each Society so petitioning shall agree to and subscribe in a Book the following five Articles, without which no agreement or Union of men upon pretence of Religious Worship shall entitle them to be incorporated and *esteemed as a Church of the Established Religion of this Commonwealth.*

First, That there is one Eternal God and a future State of Rewards and punishments.

Secondly, That God is publickly to be Worshiped.

Thirdly, That the Christian Religion is the true Religion.

Fourthly, That the Holy Scriptures of the old and new Testament are of divine inspiration, and are the only rule of Faith.

Fifthly, That it is the duty of every Man, when thereunto called by those who Govern, to bear witness to truth.[10]

The bill then goes on to try to appease the more demo-cratically-minded dissenters by stating that the people may elect their own teachers, pastors, or clergy, but that to safe-guard the state such teachers and ministers must conduct their services and their own personal lives in such a way as to set Christian examples to their congregations.

It is extremely important to note the underlying assumptions of the above passages as follows:

(1) Religion is the only basis for morality, is essential to the public welfare, and therefore should be encouraged by the state. To this end the Christian religion should be the established religion of the state.

(2) "Free exercise" of religion (within the limits defined by law) is to be tolerated.

(3) *All* Christian denominations are to be treated *equally* and *impartially* by the state and are to be recognized as a part of the established religion of the state. "Establish-ment of religion" clearly covers *all* Christian denomina-tions, not just one church. "Establishment" has come to mean multiple establishment.

(4) The state has the right to define the religious beliefs which entitle any group to be considered a part of the establishment. At this stage of the conservatives' effort it was clear that they were still ruling out Catholics, Quakers, and other small dissenting groups as well as Jews and all other non-Christian religious groups.

(5) The state should "co-operate" with all established churches in achieving the foregoing aims by providing tax support appropriately to all churches.

The bill provides as follows for the use of the taxing and enforcement machinery of the state "for the support of re-ligious teachers and places of worship." Each person must enroll his name with the county clerk and indicate which religious group he wishes to support; this listing is binding until the person chooses to select another. The county clerk then presents the lists of names to the trustees of each religious society who determine the rate of assessment on the property on the enrollees. The sheriff then collects the assessment and pays the funds to the clergymen or teachers designated by the trustees. If any person does not list his tithable (property subject to tax), the sheriff must collect the assessment anyway and pay it to the appropriate religious society. If any person fails to enroll himself as a member of any religious society, the sheriff nevertheless shall collect the assessment and divide it proportionately among all the religious groups of the community. If any established church does not appoint someone to receive the assessment, the county court divides such funds equally among the other established churches of the county. This amounts to general taxation for religion.

This was the conservatives' definition of "establishment of religion." It plainly meant multiple establishment. It was their effort to retain a hold on the privileges of the state by broadening the meaning of establishment to include all the other "respectable" religious groups. The close similarity between this Virginia bill of 1779 and the South Carolina Constitution of 1778 is immediately apparent. The Virginia bill, however, included *all Christians* in the multiple establishment whereas the South Carolina Constitution had included only all *Protestant* Christians. Thus, another step in the broadening of the meaning of establishment had been taken by the Virginia conservatives. At this stage of the struggle, however, the conservatives could not achieve their goals to widen the basis of establishment, nor could the liberals achieve their goals of separation as completely as Jefferson's bill would have done. Meanwhile, a bill to dissolve all vestries was defeated in 1779, but a year later a modified bill to dissolve several specific vestries in certain counties was passed. The liberals had made some headway. Also in 1779 a bill to preserve the property of the Church of England forever for its exclusive use was also defeated. Thus the decisive struggle over church properties and over general assessment was postponed for five years until the Revolutionary War had been fought and won.

Meanwhile, in the intervening years, Jefferson continued to state his position in favor of separation of church and state, a position based upon guarantees of free exercise of religion and upon prohibition of compulsory tax support for any religious worship. His *Notes on the State of Virginia* written in 1781-1782 contain a clear exposition of these views.[11] Jefferson had always been dissatisfied with the Virginia Constitution of 1776, so in 1783 he wrote another proposed draft of a constitution for Virginia in which the article on religion continued his consistent position in a direct line from his proposal of 1776 and 1779 in these words:

The general assembly shall not have the power to infringe this constitution; to abridge the civil rights of any person on account of his religious belief; to restrain him for professing and supporting that belief, *or to compel him to contributions,* other than those he shall have personally stipulated *for the support of that or any other;* . . . .[12]

Opposition to general assessment and multiple establishment shines through every word of this statement. Compulsory state support for any religion, even one's own religion, was a consistent object of attack by Jefferson. Never did he admit the right of the state to aid all religions equally. From 1776 on, he always knew that multiple establishment stood in the way of genuine religious freedom.

In 1784 the issues over church properties and general assessment came up again in substantially the same form, but this time with some modifications. The strength of the conservatives had grown in the Assembly following the war, and they were determined to push through a decision on both issues.

To settle the matter of glebe lands and church property, a bill for incorporating the Episcopal Church was introduced into the Assembly. The bill for incorporation would have given perpetual title of all the property of the old Church of England to the new Episcopal Church; it would have confined the vestries to members of the Episcopal Church rather than allow them to be elected by all the taxpayers of a parish; it would have given title of all property to the ministers and vestries of the church; the church could regulate its own concerns by means of general conventions consisting of two delegates from each parish, of which the minister was always to be one (thus the clergy could never be outvoted).

The other move of the conservatives was to revive the idea of multiple establishment which had been put forward in the religious bill of 1779. In 1784 Patrick Henry vigorously supported multiple establishment as embodied in the Bill Establishing a Provision for Teachers of the Christian Religion. The purpose of the assessment bill of 1784 was in Patrick Henry's words clearly to require all persons

. . . to pay a moderate tax or contribution annually for the support of the Christian religion, or of *some Christian church, denomination or communion of Christians, or for some form of Christian worship.*[13]

This meant, of course, that the conservatives were trying to maintain the privileges of the old single establishment by including all other Christian groups within a new multiple establishment on a basis of equality and impartiality. The preamble to the assessment bill asserts that the intention of the Virginia Declaration of Rights of 1776 could "be preserved by abolishing all distinctions of pre-eminence amongst the different societies or communities of Christians."[14]

Thus, the conservatives were trying to argue that the intention of Madison's article on religion in the Virginia Declaration of Rights where he said "all men are equally entitled to the free exercise of religion, according to the dictates of conscience" would be fulfilled so long as the state treated and supported all Christian churches equally. They argued that free exercise was preserved even if the state co-operated with all religions, just so it gave no preferences. The bill then went on to propose a levy on all persons to be collected by the sheriff who was to make up and post publicly a list of all taxpayers along with the religious society to which each taxpayer wished his taxes to go "for the inspection of all concerned." The sheriff then was to pay the minister or teacher so designated his share of the tax funds. If any taxpayer did not indicate a choice among the churches, his money was to be given to "seminaries of learning" within the respective counties. All money was to be used for paying clergymen or religious teachers or providing places of divine worship, except that Quakers and Mennonites could use it for *any* purpose they desired.

Thus, the base of the establishment was now to be still broader than that of the bill of 1779 which had set up definite and elaborate stipulations defining a church eligible to receive funds and which had effectively limited such churches to the major Protestant denominations. Now, however, the assessment bill of 1784 did not lay down such restrictions and apparently included *all* Christians, the small radical sects as well as Catholics, but no non-Christians as yet. Indeed, the Assembly almost took the final step of multiple establishment to include *all* religious groups equally and impartially. In the debates on the assessment bill on December 22 and 23, 1784 the Assembly in committee of the whole voted by a small majority to substitute the word "religious" for "Christian." This would have levied an assessment "for the support of religious teachers," but in report to the house the conservatives were able to reverse the decision and re-insert "Christian," thus ruling out the non-Christian religious groups. But for this close decision, the assessment bill would have arrived at exactly the proposals now being made for the state to support all religions equally and impartially (see the third alternative, 3b, multiple establishment, p. 8 above). As it was, the bill as actually framed is substantially the same in principle, involving co-operation between the state and all major churches in order to promote religious instruction.

Madison saw these implications of the assessment bill and exerted all his efforts to defeat it. He made a notable speech in opposition to Patrick Henry's defense of the assessment bill. This speech of Madison's is not preserved in full but his notes for it clearly reveal that he considered the assessment bill a proposal for "an establishment of religion."[15] He uses the very word "establishment" throughout, and his main intent was to point out that the issue was *not* whether religion was necessary but whether religious establishments were necessary for religion. He, of course, insisted that they were not. He asserted that the true cause of the decline of morality was not a lessening of religion but the results of the war, unjust laws, corrupt court practices, and the transition period from war to peace. He insisted that the true remedies for the decline in morality were not to establish religion but to improve the laws, create a better administration of justice, engage in voluntary associations for religion through personal effort, and educate youth.

It is clear that Madison did not mean the education of youth by religious teachers, because that was the exact intent of the assessment bill which he was opposing so bitterly. The "seminaries of learning" mentioned in the assessment bill were taught by the clergy and housed in the churches or in the glebe houses and supported by tuition. Indeed, one of the reasons for promoting the assessment bill was doubtless to bolster the declining income of religious teachers by gaining a share of public funds for religious education. At least so Madison believed.[16] The parallels between the struggle over assessment in Virginia and the recent struggles described in Chapter 6 are so striking that all Americans should be well aware of the issues involved and should be prepared to accept the responsibility for returning to the conservative assessment proposals of 165 years ago if they should so decide. The essence of these proposals is to use public tax funds for promoting religious instruction.

The assessment bill stirred up enormous public feeling throughout Virginia and divided the state as few issues ever did. Petitions and memorials came to the legislature by the dozens. A thorough study of these petitions and their supporting arguments[17] shows clearly the agitated state of mind of hundreds of citizens. Up to the end of December, 1784 the weight of opinion as expressed in the petitions favored assessment as well as the incorporation bill. In fact, Madison decided not to oppose the incorporation bill for fear that stubborn resistance would enable the conservatives to drive through the assessment bill too. So, viewing the assessment bill as the greater evil, he voted for the incorporation bill which was passed on December 22, 1784. Then, marshalling his forces against the assessment bill, he was able to persuade the Assembly to postpone the final reading of the assessment bill until the next session of the Assembly in November, 1785, nearly a year later. Thereupon, the Assembly voted to have the assessment bill engrossed and distributed throughout the state with a request to the people to register their opinion of it by the next session. Madison was willing and anxious to rest his case with the will of the people of the whole state.

In order to carry his case to the people Madison wrote his famous *Memorial and Remonstrance Against Religious Assessments*[18] which was widely distributed during the summer of 1785. The *Remonstrance* is Madison's most complete statement of what he understood the conservatives to mean by "an establishment of religion." It is unequivocally clear that he identified the assessment proposal to aid all religious groups equally, as "an establishment of religion," as did the proponents of the bill, no less in 1785 than in 1779. It reveals clearly that he opposed any kind of connection between church and state, that he opposed multiple support for *all* churches as vigorously as he opposed the establishment of a single church. Some of his major arguments against the assessment bill are as follows:

He quoted from his article on religion in the Virginia Declaration of Rights and then insisted that this meant that every man has an inalienable right to the freedom of his individual conscience. This right cannot be subjected to the authority of civil society nor to the legislature of the state.

The Religion then of every man must be left to the conviction and conscience of every man; and it is the right of every man to exercise it as these may dictate. This right is in its nature an unalienable right. . . . We maintain therefore that in matters of Religion, no man's right is abridged by the institution of Civil Society, and that Religion is wholly exempt from its cognizance.[19]

Free exercise of religion must rest upon this natural right and not upon the pleasure of the state.

Who does not see that the same authority which can establish Christianity, in exclusion of all other Religions, may establish with the same ease any particular sect of Christians, in exclusion of all other Sects? That the same authority which can force a citizen to contribute three pence only of his property for the support of any one establishment, may force him to conform to any other establishment in all cases whatsoever?[20]

It is not the amount of assessment that matters, it is the *principle* of establishment that is wrong. Public taxation for the Christian religion in general is as wrong as public taxation for a single preferred sect.

The next major point is that *equality* before the law is an essential civil right, of which religious conscience is the primary civil right. Free exercise of religion must be based upon equal rights of conscience, both of which the assessment bill violates by subjecting some to peculiar burdens and others to peculiar exemptions.

If "all men are by nature equally free and independent," [Virginia Declaration of Rights, Article I] all men are to be considered as entering into Society on equal conditions; as relinquishing no more, and therefore retaining no less, one than another, of their natural rights. Above all they are to be considered as retaining an *"equal title to the free exercise of Religion according to the dictates of conscience."* [Article 16] Whilst we assert for ourselves a freedom to embrace, to profess, and to observe the Religion which we believe to be of divine origin, we cannot deny an equal freedom to those whose minds have not yet yielded to the evidence which has convinced us.[21]

Here, in these ringing statements, Madison rests his case for religious freedom upon the basic American doctrines of freedom and equality as inalienable civil rights. Madison's last sentence may well include the right of any individual *not* to believe in any particular religious doctrine or in any religious doctrine at all.

In the next point he echoes Roger Williams' inevitable conclusion that the state has no right to define what is or what is not an appropriate religious belief for anyone:

. . . the bill implies either that the Civil Magistrate is a competent Judge of Religious truth; or that he may employ Religion as an engine of Civil policy.[22]

This is the predicament any society creates when the state tries to "co-operate" with any one church or with all churches impartially, for the state will inevitably have to make distinctions among religious beliefs if it sets out to encourage or support any or all of them.

Madison goes on to make several historical arguments to give further weight to his arguments on principle: ". . . the establishment proposed by the Bill is not requisite for the support of the Christian Religion" and "the establishment in question is not necessary for the support of Civil Government." Religion has flourished more freely where there have been no establishments, and civil rights have been more secure where there have been no religious establishments. Such an establishment will warn immigrants away from what they thought was a haven for the religiously persecuted, and it will drive present good citizens away from the state. The bill for establishment will fan the flames of religious intolerance and divide the community along religious lines, whereas complete religious freedom enables everyone to live in civil harmony. Finally, if the legislature can infringe this most fundamental of the civil rights, it may with impunity go on to control the freedom of the press, abolish trial by jury, or even take away the very rights of suffrage. All rights secured by the Virginia Constitution will be in jeopardy, and thus the legislature has no constitutional right to pass the assessment bill.

This is Madison's definitive statement of the arguments against establishment of religion as he interpreted the assessment bill directly in the light of the meaning of the Virginia Declaration of Rights and Constitution. The continuity of Madison's thinking is incontestable when one studies the speeches he made in the first Congress of 1789 when he introduced his proposals for a bill of rights as amendments to the Constitution of the United States (see pages 78-85). These were the basic arguments and principles that shaped his thinking as he guided the First Amendment and the other amendments through the congressional debates. Jefferson heartily approved Madison's arguments.[23]

With the *Remonstrance* as the common underlying principle for action the people of Virginia during the summer and fall of 1785 flooded the legislature with petitions and memorials opposing assessment. The response was so overwhelming that the assessment bill was never brought to a vote. It also had such effect in the elections to the new session of the legislature that Madison and the liberals were in so great a majority that they had no trouble in bringing up Jefferson's Bill for Religious Freedom of 1779 and passing it by the overwhelming majority of 74 to 20 in January 1786. This then became the historic Virginia Statute of Religious Freedom (see page 52). The next year the liberals turned their attention to the incorporation bill and easily repealed it in January of 1787. On the eve of the Constitutional Convention the separation of church and state had been completed in Virginia.[24]

One final word on the struggle in Virginia. Such an overwhelming victory could not have been won without the support of many members of the Episcopal Church as well as of the dissenting groups. Perhaps the best example of the attitude of many adherents of the old establishment was George Washington, himself for long a vestryman of the Church of England. In a letter to George Mason who had sent him a copy of Madison's *Remonstrance,* Washington revealed his sentiments as follows:

Altho, no man's sentiments are more opposed to *any kind* of restraint upon religious principles than mine are; yet I must confess, that I am not amongst the number of those who are so much alarmed at the thoughts of making people pay towards the support of that which they profess, if of the denomination of Christians; or declare themselves Jews, Mahomitans or otherwise, and thereby obtain proper relief. As the matter now stands, I wish an assessment had never been agitated, and as it has gone so far, that the Bill could die an easy death; because I think it will be productive of more quiet to the State, than by enacting it into a Law; which, in my opinion, would be impolitic, admitting there is a decided majority for it, to the disquiet of a respectable minority. In the first case the matter will soon subside; in the latter, it will rankle and perhaps convulse, the State.[25]

Here it is plain that Washington saw no particular objection to assessment on religious grounds, but his loyalty to complete religious freedom as a protection for the common welfare of the State led him to oppose the assessment bill. No one was more outspoken in his belief in the importance of religion as a fundamental human good, but if any form of establishment were to divide the community or "convulse the state" then the common welfare must come first and establishment must go. To set up the public welfare of the community as the test for such a moral judgment is a basically secular test. In view of his deep religious convictions concerning the value of religious freedom, Washington came to agree with Madison and Jefferson that the value of religious establishments must be subjected to the secular test of the public welfare as well as to the religious test of equality of conscience. More and more conservatives as well as liberals, reluctantly or willingly, came to the same conclusion. Upon such common agreements the principle of separation of church and state firmly rested among most of the states in the early National period.

Although the struggle for separation of church and state was perhaps more spectacular and thoroughgoing in Virginia than elsewhere, the trend was so evident between 1776 and 1791 that disestablishment was definitely the will of a large majority of states by the time the First Amendment was framed and adopted. By 1791 it is clear that virtual separation had already been achieved in the constitutions of nine of the original thirteen states. Despite differences of wording in these nine constitutions,[26] several show unmistakable similarity in wording and all show a basic similarity in purpose and meaning, namely, the protection of free exercise of worship, prohibition of preference to any one or several religious groups, and prohibition of support for any religious worship or instruction.

In only four states after 1791 did the constitutions still permit the use of public funds for the support of religious worship and ministers. These states were Maryland and the three New England states of Massachusetts, Connecticut and New Hampshire. Although laws were gradually enacted in these states to do away with compulsory support as the last stronghold of establishment, this movement did not appear in the constitutions of these states until 1810 in Maryland, 1818 in Connecticut, and 1833 in Massachusetts.[27]

The situation in New Hampshire remained ambiguous, for the Constitution of 1784 authorized, on one hand, the towns to provide support for "public protestant teachers of piety, religion, and morality," but on the other hand, provided that "no portion of any one particular religious sect or denomination, shall ever be compelled to pay towards the support of the teacher or teachers of another persuasion, sect or denomination." New Hampshire destroyed its multiple establishment by statute rather than by constitutional amendment when the legislature passed a law in 1819 depriving the towns of the power to levy taxes for the support of religion. New Hampshire's Constitution had *permitted* the legislature to authorize the towns to support religion and had not *required* the legislature to do so, as in Massachusetts. This permissive provision still remains in the New Hampshire Constitution, but separation was achieved by statute as in Virginia.

Vermont's situation was also ambiguous. Vermont's constitutions of 1777 and 1786, before admission to the Union, had ruled out compulsory support for religion. The constitution of 1793, after admission in 1791, contained similar provisions, but in 1783 Vermont had passed a law permitting towns to vote to establish a minister or ministers. This permissive law was abrogated by a law of 1807 which deprived the towns of the power to support ministers or build meeting-houses by levying taxes. Vermont's laws were thus brought into conformity with the state constitution.

Despite the delay in modifying the constitutions of these states the fact is that at the time of the framing of the First Amendment the majority outlook in America was definitely in favor of the essential principles of separation of church and state, as defined so clearly in Virginia.

4

The Principle of Separation in the Nation

THE FORMAL CREATION of a new nation in America took place in a period of transition when ideas and practices concerning the relation between church and state were undergoing drastic change. Free exercise of religion had been formally won in all states by 1789; establishments of single churches had been effectively challenged and destroyed by constitutional or legislative enactment; and efforts were being made to broaden establishments of religion to include many sects on a basis of impartiality. Indeed the only battles remaining to be fought were those concerned with financial support by the state of the four remaining multiple establishments. It was in this setting that the principle of separation of church and state was eventually to be enunciated in the constitutional law of the new nation.

At the beginning of its life, in 1774, the Continental Congress reflected current attitudes of respect for religion and reliance upon religious sanctions for aid in the common effort. Chaplains were appointed to conduct prayers for the Congress, and chaplains of a variety of faiths were assigned to the Revolutionary armies in the field. These developments doubtless represented not only a desire to meet the spiritual needs of the soldiers, but also a recognition that the common effort of soldiers of all faiths was necessary for the successful prosecution of the war. These religious practices grew out of the desire to enlist the various religious groups into a common effort for the general welfare.

At the conclusion of the Revolutionary War, Congress revealed that it thought of itself as strictly limited in its functions in matters of religion. In 1783 the Papal Nuncio in Paris asked Benjamin Franklin if the Congress would permit the establishment of a Catholic Bishop in America, but the Congress replied to Franklin,

the subject . . . being purely spiritual, it is without the jurisdiction and powers of Congress, who have no authority to permit or refuse it, these powers being reserved to the several states individually.[1]

This action, reflecting a reluctance by Congress to assert itself on matters of religion, was soon to be replaced, however, by later actions in which Congress attempted to become somewhat more directive on religious affairs.

When the Land Ordinance of 1785 was being framed, the religious problem came to the fore again. When the states gave up their claims to the western lands and handed them over to the general government, Congress was faced with developing a policy by which the public land was to be surveyed and sold. There was a conflict between the "New England plan" (whereby whole townships were to be sold in one piece after survey) and the "Virginia plan" (whereby individuals could first settle on parcels of the land and then proceed to determine matters of boundary afterwards). A committee of Congress headed by Jefferson proposed a plan in 1785 which contained no reference to education or to religion, but it was not acted upon. A new committee, consisting of representatives of all thirteen states, but not including Jefferson, who was in Europe, drew up a proposal for the Ordinance of 1785 in which the "New England plan" dominated.

In this draft it was originally proposed that the sixteenth section of each township be set aside for the use of public schools and another section to be used for the support of the ministry, according to the practice of town establishment current in Massachusetts and Connecticut. In the course of committee action the proposal for support of the ministry was defeated,[2] and thus only the sixteenth section for public schools was retained in the final version of the Ordinance of 1785. It is clear that if the New Englanders had had their way the Ordinance of 1785 might have embodied a part of the New England form of multiple religious establishment. Upon hearing of the committee's action, Madison revealed his relief in a letter to James Monroe that the religious clause had been defeated:

> How a regulation so unjust in itself, so foreign to the Authority of Congs, so hurtful to the sale of the public land, and smelling so strongly of an antiquated Bigotry, could have received the countenance of a Comtee is truly a matter of astonishment.[3]

Madison went on to indicate that such a support for religion in the new territory would have achieved the same results of encroachment upon religious liberty that would have occurred in Virginia if the assessment bill had passed. He thus identified both efforts as religious establishments that would have prevented genuine religious freedom.

Later, when the Northwest Ordinance of 1787 was framed, it also revealed the New England attitude toward religion, which combined a desire for religious freedom with encouragement of religion by the government. The Northwest Ordinance was largely the work of Nathan Dane, Rufus King, and Rev. Manassah Cutler, all from Massachusetts. It reflected their desire to establish the civil liberties of religious freedom, trial by jury, habeas corpus, and prohibition of slavery as encouragements to migration and the sale of land; it also reflected their desire to encourage religion in the famous article, "Religion, morality and knowledge, being necessary to good government and the happiness of mankind, schools and the means of education shall forever be encouraged."

The Northwest Ordinance was passed by Congress in July 1787 while many of its members were attending the Constitutional Convention in Philadelphia. When Cutler and others received great tracts of land for the Ohio Company, they received land for the support of religion (section 29) as well as for schools (section 16); so did John C. Symmes in his grant. The federal government had not yet reflected fully the trends toward separation of church and state that were under way in many of the states. It is significant, however, that after the Constitution and the First Amendment were adopted, no more public land was granted for the support of religion under the ordinance.[4]

From what we know of the deliberations of the Constitutional Convention in 1787, very little was said about religion. Interestingly enough, however, Madison's journal of the proceedings contains a draft of a constitution by Charles Pinckney of South Carolina in which the following provision appears in the list of prohibitions upon the powers of Congress:

. . . the Legislature of the United States shall pass no law on the subject of religion; nor touching or abridging the liberty of the press; nor shall the privilege of the writ of Habeas Corpus ever be suspended, except in case of rebellion or invasion.[5]

It is now authenticated, however, that this draft by Pinckney was not presented to the Convention, but for some reason was later inserted in Madison's journal.[6] In any case the draft of a constitution, presented by a Committee of Detail on August 6, 1787 contained no clauses on religion or freedom of the press, although a clause on habeas corpus did appear and was retained. In a later discussion of the draft Pinckney proposed this addition:

... but no religious test shall ever be required as a qualification to any office or public trust under the authority of the United States.

After some discussion this clause was adopted and became a part of Article VI of the Constitution.

The Convention was apparently willing to outlaw religious discrimination among federal office holders but not at this stage to prohibit religious establishments as a protection for the equal rights of conscience. But the people of several of the states were not satisfied with this partial achievement. New York, Virginia, and New Hampshire ratified the Constitution but proposed amendments for a bill of rights, specifically including religious freedom and disestablishment. North Carolina and Rhode Island would not ratify until a bill of rights, including religion, was adopted. The "public clamor" for a more thoroughgoing separation of church and state was so great that Madison and others could persuade several states to adopt the Constitution as framed at the Convention only after promising to work for the addition of amendments that would genuinely protect civil liberties in a specific bill of rights in which freedom and equality of religious conscience played a prominent and fundamental part.

Madison's zeal for promising that a bill of rights would be added *after* the Constitution was ratified was no doubt strengthened by Jefferson's outlook which was clearly stated in a letter to Madison on December 20, 1787. Excerpts from this letter are quoted at length because they show how strongly Jefferson felt that the fundamental rights of all men, including religion, must be protected by bills of rights in both the federal and state constitutions:

I will now add what I do not like [about the Constitution as framed]. First, the omission of a bill of rights providing clearly & without the aid of sophisms for freedom of religion, freedom of the press, protection against standing armies, restriction against monopolies, the eternal & unremitting force of the habeas corpus laws, and trials by juries in all matters of fact triable by the laws of the land & not by the law of nations. To say, as Mr. Wilson does that a bill of rights was not necessary because all is reserved in the case of the general government which is not given, while in the particular ones all is given which is not reserved, might do for the audience to whom it was addressed, but is surely a *gratis dictum,* opposed by strong inferences from the body of the instrument. . . . It would have been much more just & wise to have concluded the other way that as most of the states had judiciously preserved this palladium [trial by jury], those who had wandered should be brought back to it, and to have established general right instead of general wrong. Let me add that *a bill of rights is what the people are entitled to against every government on earth, general or particular, & what no just government should refuse, or rest on inferences.*[7]

Jefferson thus reiterated his belief that religious freedom was one of the basic civil rights along with freedom of speech, trial by jury, and the rights of habeas corpus. His comments about trial by jury could just as well have been made concerning freedom of religion as a right that should be protected in a bill of rights for the federal or "general" government just as in bills of rights for the state or "particular" governments. Throughout his writings Jefferson used the phrase "freedom of religion" to include freedom from compulsory taxation for the support of religion as well as freedom of exercise of religious worship and belief. This civil right should be mutually protected in similar bills of rights in the federal and state constitutions. Both should give the same protection in similar terms. Jefferson had already indicated how a state should protect religious rights by his activities and proposals for the Virginia Constitution. He believed that the United States Constitution should contain a bill of rights protecting the same civil liberties that he had fought for in Virginia. Just as Virginia must not prohibit the free exercise of religion nor enforce compulsory support of any religion, so the United States must not prohibit the free exercise of religion nor enforce compulsory support of any religion.

Despite Jefferson's long advocacy of the rights of the states as against the federal government, he was convinced that "states' rights" did not extend to the right to take away any of the "natural rights" of men. No person would have a right to religious freedom under a state government if the federal government had the right to take it away; conversely, no person would have a right to religious freedom under the federal government if a state had the right to take it away. Therefore, neither the federal government nor the state governments should have the right to prohibit the free exercise of religion or to require compulsory support for any religion by single or multiple establishment. Those states that have "wandered" from religious freedom should be brought back to it. Thus, in Jefferson's view, the federal and state governments should be uniform in their protection of the civil liberties of religion, press, trial by jury, and habeas corpus.

On October 17, 1788, Madison wrote to Jefferson, sending him a set of proposals for amendment to the Constitution which was then in process of being ratified by the several states. In this letter Madison stated his own questions at that time concerning the value of a written bill of rights. Madison's overpowering purpose was to get the Constitution ratified, and he was sometimes afraid that if too many states delayed ratification on the grounds that no bill of rights was included, the whole project of a new constitution would be lost. His main concern was to get ratification and *then* turn to a bill of rights. In this letter he stated his position to Jefferson as follows:

My own opinion has always been in favor of a bill of rights; provided it be so framed as not to imply powers not meant to be included in the enumeration.

At the same time I have never thought the omission a material defect, nor been anxious to supply it even by *subsequent* [italics

Madison's] amendment, for any other reason than that it is anxiously desired by others. I have favored it because I supposed it might be of use, and if properly executed could not be of disservice. I have not viewed it in an important light — 1. because I conceive that in a certain degree, though not in the extent argued by Mr. Wilson, the rights in question are reserved by the manner in which the federal powers are granted. 2. because there is great reason to fear that a positive declaration of some of the most essential rights could not be obtained *in the requisite latitude. I am sure that the rights of conscience in particular,* if submitted to public definition *would be narrowed much more* than they are likely ever to be by an assumed power. One of the objections in New England was that the Constitution by prohibiting religious tests, opened a door for Jews, Turks, & infidels. 3. because the limited powers of the federal government and the jealousy of the subordinate Governments, afford a security which has not existed in the case of the State Governments, and exists in no other; 4. because experience proves the inefficacy of a bill of rights on those occasions when its control is most needed. Repeated violations of these parchment barriers have been committed by overbearing majorities in every State. In Virginia I have seen the bill of rights violated in every instance where it has been opposed to a popular current. *Notwithstanding the explicit provision contained in that instrument for the rights of Conscience, it is well known that a religious establishment would have taken place in that State,* if the Legislative majority had found as they expected, a majority of the people in favor of the measure; and I am persuaded that if a majority of the people were now of one sect, the measure would still take place and on *narrower ground than was then proposed,* notwithstanding the additional obstacle which the law has since created.[8]

Two points in this letter are especially noteworthy. The first is that Madison was afraid that a written guarantee of religious freedom would not be interpreted broadly enough to permit as full protection for the rights of conscience as he desired. This helps to explain why, in the first Congress, Madison steadily fought to make the First Amendment as broad as possible in meaning and constantly opposed all efforts to limit its application to a single establishment (see pages

78-91). The second point in his unmistakable reference to the assessment bill in Virginia when he said that "a religious establishment would have taken place in that State" in violation of the Virginia Constitution. He could not have been referring in these words to the single establishment of the Church of England, for a preference for one church would have been an establishment "on narrower grounds." Here was further notice that a prohibition against broad (or multiple) establishments would be necessary in the federal bill of rights, not simply a limited prohibition against a single establishment.

Madison went on to say in the above letter that the invasion of rights in a popular government is likely to come from the majority against the minority in the community rather than from the government itself and then summed up his position in favor of a bill of rights as follows:

> What use then it may be asked can a bill of rights serve in popular Governments? I answer the two following which, though less essential than in other Governments [monarchies], sufficiently recommend the precaution: 1. The political truths declared in that solemn manner acquire by degrees the character of fundamental maxims of free Government, and as they become incorporated with the national sentiment, counteract the impulses of interest and passion. 2. Although it be generally true as above stated that the danger of oppression lies in the interested majorities of the people rather than in usurped acts of the Government, yet there may be occasions on which the evil may spring from the latter source; and on such, a bill of rights will be a good ground for an appeal to the sense of the community.[9]

Despite his reservations concerning a particular bill of rights, Madison *was* definitely in favor of such a bill, and this apparently lukewarm attitude toward a bill of rights was soon changed. Madison had been so anxious to get Virginia to ratify the Constitution as it stood that the rumor began to go about that he was not only opposed to amendments but had given up his loyalty to religious freedom. Since he was to be a member of the new House of Representatives from his district, he was prompted to explain the change from his earlier views. This he did in a letter of January 2, 1789:

I freely own that I have never seen in the Constitution as it now stands those serious dangers which have alarmed many respectable citizens. Accordingly whilst it remained unratified, and it was necessary to unite the States in some one plan, I opposed all previous alterations as calculated to throw the States into dangerous contentions, and to furnish the secret enemies of the Union with an opportunity of promoting its dissolution. *Circumstances are now changed.* The Constitution is established on the ratifications of eleven States and a very great majority of the people of America; and amendments, if pursued with a proper moderation and in a proper mode, will be not only safe, but may serve the double purpose of satisfying the minds of well meaning opponents, and of providing additional guards in favor of liberty. *Under this change of circumstances, it is my sincere opinion that the Constitution ought to be revised, and that the first Congress* meeting under it ought to prepare and recommend to the States for ratification, the most satisfactory provisions for all essential rights, *particularly the rights of Conscience in the fullest latitude,* the freedom of the press, trial by jury, security against general warrants, etc.[10]

His first mission accomplished, the Constitution ratified and the Union established, Madison was ready to devote wholehearted attention to amendments embodying a bill of rights. This resolve was no doubt strengthened by Jefferson's constant urging that a bill of rights should be a part of the Constitution. On March 15, 1789, just after Madison went to the House of Representatives, Jefferson wrote him from Paris, replying to the four questions about a bill of rights as raised by Madison's letter to Jefferson of October 17, 1788 quoted above. Jefferson felt that such questions were not strong enough to stand in the way of the greater values of a written bill of rights. In the course of his arguments Jefferson referred to his proposed draft of a constitution for Virginia in 1783 as containing his conceptions of "all the great objects of public liberty."[11] In this context of discussing the United States Constitution Jefferson was unmistakably indicating that his desires for religious freedom and civil liberty in Virginia were applicable to the federal Constitution. It will be remembered that Jefferson's proposed constitution for Virginia in 1783 contained a prohibition against compulsory support for one's own or any other religious belief. Within three months after this letter was written Madison was displaying a similar outlook and determination as he set about his efforts to achieve a bill of rights eventually to be headed by the First Amendment.

The First Amendment

On March 3, 1789 the first Congress assembled under the new Constitution, and three months later James Madison introduced into the House of Representatives his compilation of proposals for amendments to the Constitution to meet the demands for a declaration of rights. In a notable speech on June 8, 1789 Madison marshalled his arguments for approving a bill of rights and listed in detail the specific rights to be included. Madison insisted throughout his speech that the rights he named should be protected not only because of their inherent importance but also because of the political strength that would be added to the new government by meeting the demands of large numbers of people for specific mention of such rights in the Constitution.[12] Prominent in his proposals were the religious clauses, and it is clear that he counted religious freedom and disestablishment as among the two or three most important civil rights to be protected.

In the light of recent efforts to reinterpret what the First Amendment meant to the people of the country and to the members of the First Congress in the period from 1789 until adoption of the First Amendment in 1791, it is important to follow carefully the course of the debates that surrounded the religious clauses of the First Amendment. The "plain meaning" of the wording of the First Amendment cannot be divorced from the struggles that had been going on in the states from 1776 onward nor from the experience and intent of Madison, Jefferson, and others who had been in the thick of these struggles.

In his speech of June 8 Madison clearly revealed his intentions in the two basic proposals he made with respect to religion. He saw the problem as twofold: (1) the federal government must not establish religion and must not infringe the equal rights of conscience or the free exercise of religion; on the other hand, (2) the states must also be prohibited from infringing the rights of conscience. In all the debates of Congress this twofold approach of Madison should be kept in mind, and it should be remembered that the House of Representatives *voted to put restrictions upon the states as well as upon Congress.* Apparently the Senate was not willing to limit the states in this way, but it was Madison's intention all along to make this double-barrelled approach to separation of church and state. He would have separated establishments of religion from the state governments as well as from the federal government, and the House of Representatives agreed with him. If the Senate had concurred in 1789 many of the later difficulties might not have arisen and some of the reasons for the Fourteenth Amendment would have been obviated.

Madison's two original proposals were as follows. Madison proposed to insert in Article I, Section 9 of the Constitution, among those clauses that put limitations upon the powers of Congress, these words:

> The civil rights of none shall be abridged on account of religious belief or worship, nor shall any national religion be established, nor shall the full and equal rights of conscience be in any manner, or on any pretext, infringed.[13]

The continuity of ideas, intent, and wording between this proposal and Madison's work in Virginia is clear. His use of the words "national religion" in this section is also easily explained, because he immediately follows with his proposal to limit the powers of the states as well. He proposed to insert in Article I, Section 10 of the Constitution, where limitations were put upon the powers of the states, the following words:

> No State shall violate the equal rights of conscience, or the freedom of the press, or the trial by jury in criminal cases.[14]

Now, some recent writers have been trying to prove that Madison was simply trying to prevent the establishment of a single national church, that he was *not* interested in preventing co-operation between the federal government and religion, and that he was willing to let the states be free to set up any form of established religion that they might wish. It is clear, however, from a thorough study of Madison's efforts in Virginia as well as from his proposals and arguments in the First Congress that he saw the problem much more broadly. Indeed, he did not want a single national church established but his use of the formula "equal rights of conscience" was clearly intended to prevent *all* forms of single or multiple establishment as well as to prevent "co-operation" between the states or the federal government and any or all churches. His *Remonstrance* against assessment in Virginia in 1786 is of a single piece with his speech of June 8, 1789 in Congress.

Throughout his speech in Congress Madison refers again and again to liberty of conscience, freedom of the press, and trial by jury as *the* great rights of the people. Not only must these rights be protected from encroachment by the executive and legislative branches of government, but also these rights of the minority must be protected against the majority in the community. In his supporting arguments describing the rights which the federal government may not infringe, Madison made this point as follows:

> But whatever may be the form which the several States have adopted in making declarations in favor of particular rights, the great object in view is to limit and qualify the powers of Govern-

ment, by excepting out of the grant of power those cases in which the Government ought not to act, or to act only in a particular mode. They point these exceptions sometimes against the abuse of the executive power, sometimes against the legislative, and, in some cases, against the community itself; or, in other words, against the majority in favor of the minority. . . .

But I confess that I do conceive, that in a Government modified like this of the United States, the great danger lies rather in the abuse of the community than in the legislative body. The prescriptions in favor of liberty ought to be levelled against that quarter where the greatest danger lies, namely, that which possesses the highest prerogative of power. But this is not found in either the executive or legislative departments of Government, but in the body of the people, operating by the majority against the minority.[15]

This argument surely means with respect to religion that, even if the majority of people hold to a certain religious belief, they have no right to violate the equal rights of conscience of the minority nor to use the power of government to support the majority's view.[16] Even if the majority in America is Christian, the government may not be used to aid the Christian religion in violation of the conscience of non-Christian minorities. "Co-operation" of majority churches with the state is prohibited by the constitutional and civil rights of conscience.

In two further statements Madison unequivocally indicates that the federal government's stand on the bill of rights will be effective upon the whole nation and upon the states. One way this will happen is by example:

If they [the bill of rights] are incorporated into the constitution, independent tribunals of justice will consider themselves in a peculiar manner the guardians of those rights; they will be an impenetrable bulwark against every assumption of power in the legislative or executive; they will be naturally led to resist every encroachment upon rights expressly stipulated for in the constitution by the declaration of rights. Besides this security, there is a great probability that such a declaration in the federal system would be enforced; because the State Legislatures will jealously and closely watch the operations of this Government, and be able to resist with more effect every assumption of power, than any other power on earth can do; and the greatest opponents to a Federal Government admit the State Legislatures to be sure guardians of the people's liberty. I conclude, from this view of the subject, that it will be proper in itself, and highly politic, for the tranquillity of the public mind, and the stability of the Government, that we should offer something, in the form I have proposed, to be incorporated in the system of Government, as a declaration of the rights of the people.[17]

A second way to influence the states is to make specific in the federal constitution that the states too are limited in their powers with respect to certain of the basic civil rights. It is noteworthy that Madison said on at least two occasions in Congress that he considered this proposal to be of an importance equal to if not greater than the limitation upon the powers of Congress:

I wish also, in revising the constitution, we may throw into that section, which interdicts the abuse of certain powers in the State Legislatures, some other provisions of equal, if not greater importance than those already made. . . . I think there is more danger of those powers being abused by the State Governments than by the Government of the United States. The same may be said of other powers which they possess, if not controlled by the general principle, that laws are unconstitutional which infringe the rights of the community. I should therefore wish to extend this interdiction, and add, as I have stated in the 5th resolution, that no State shall violate the equal right of conscience, freedom of the press, or trial by jury in criminal cases; because it is proper that every Government should be disarmed of powers which trench upon those particular rights. I know, in some of the State constitutions, the power of the Government is controlled by such a declaration; but others are not. I cannot see any reason against obtaining even a double security on those points; and nothing can give a more sincere proof of the attachment of those who opposed this constitution to these great and important rights, than to see them join in obtaining the security I have now proposed; because it must be admitted, on all hands, that the State Governments are as liable to attack these invaluable privileges as the General Government is, and therefore ought to be as cautiously guarded against.[18]

No words could more plainly show that Madison looked upon the amendments to the Constitution as a part of a continuing process that had already begun in most of the states but which should be extended to all states by the power of the United States. The Fourteenth Amendment is foreshadowed here.

After Madison's speech there was considerable debate over what to do with his proposals. At first it was voted to consider them in Committee of the Whole, but on July 21 a committee of eleven members (one from each state, including Madison) was appointed to consider the proposals and report to the House. On July 28 this committee's report was presented to the House and ordered to lie on the table. On August 13 the House resolved itself into Committee of the Whole and began debate upon the committee's report which embodied Madison's proposals with some changes. On August 15 the Committee of the Whole debated the first religious clause which the committee had shortened in wording by leaving out the reference to civil rights and the word "national." It read as follows:

. . . no religion shall be established by law, nor shall the equal rights of conscience be infringed.[19]

In the debates that followed on that day there is not a complete record of statements in the *Annals of Congress* but only a summary and synopsis rather than the actual verbatim reports of the speeches. Therefore, the problem of interpretation becomes difficult, but there is no doubt that motives were complicated and that political issues were present as they always are in constitutional debates. Madison had to chart his course among many shoals as he guided his proposed amendments to acceptance. He had to convince those who felt that the whole business of a bill of rights was dangerous or unnecessary and a waste of time; he had to win over those who believed establishment of religion was a good thing; and he had to insist upon sufficient powers for the federal government to make it an effective and strong government without making it appear too strong in the eyes of those still convinced of the necessity of sovereign states' rights.

Peter Sylvester of New York was afraid that the clause would have a tendency to abolish religion entirely. Elbridge Gerry of Massachusetts evidently thought that the clause should be narrowed down simply to free exercise of worship, for he proposed that the clause should read "no religious doctrine shall be established by law." This wording would have still permitted a New England town form of multiple establishment. Roger Sherman of Connecticut thought the clause was entirely unnecessary because "Congress had no authority whatever delegated to them by the constitution to make religious establishments. . . ." Daniel Carroll of Maryland, a Catholic, was in favor of the clause as it stood, and Madison said that "he apprehended the meaning of the words to be, that Congress should not establish a religion, and enforce the legal observation of it by law, nor compel men to worship God in any manner contrary to their conscience."[20] In the light of Madison's experience and expressed views "establish a religion" meant to him financial support for religion.

When Benjamin Huntington of Connecticut said that he feared the clause would aid those who professed no religion at all, Madison was ready to compromise to save the clause and suggested that the word "national" be inserted before "religion" in order to satisfy the reluctant members of the House. He indicated that some people feared that one sect or two sects might combine together to gain a preference and establish a religion to which they would compel others to conform. This suggestion of Madison to speak of a "national religion" was a return to his original proposals in his speech of June 8 which, it must be remembered, also included the restriction upon the states as well. Madison no doubt still hoped for passage of this second aspect of his twofold proposal when he was willing to say that Congress could not establish a "national" religion. Thereupon, Gerry said that Madison was an ultranationalist in favor of extreme powers for the national government and was overstepping the bounds of a limited "federal" government. Madison withdrew his proposal in the face of this argument, but insisted that he was not proposing extreme powers for an over-powerful national government. A revision was suggested by Samuel Livermore of New Hampshire as follows:

Congress shall make no laws touching religion, or infringing the rights of conscience.[21]

This wording, including for the first time the word "Congress," was adopted, 31 to 20. Only a simple majority was necessary to adopt a report in Committee of the Whole.

On August 17 the second half of Madison's proposals on religion came up for debate, namely, "no state shall infringe the equal rights of conscience. . . ." Thomas T. Tucker of South Carolina argued that the Congress had no right to interfere with the states and moved to strike out the whole clause. It was then that Madison replied as summarized in the *Annals of Congress* as follows:

Mr. MADISON conceived this to be the most valuable amendment in the whole list. If there was any reason to restrain the Government of the United States from infringing upon these essential rights, it was equally necessary that they should be secured against the State Governments. He thought that if they provided against the one, it was as necessary to provide against the other, and was satisfied that it would be equally grateful to the people.[22]

Livermore of New Hampshire again proposed a revision, "the equal rights of conscience, . . . shall not be infringed by any State." Tucker's motion was rejected and Livermore's adopted. (The details of the vote are not mentioned in the *Annals*.) This meant that the Committee of the Whole adopted both of Madison's proposals on religion.

On August 20 the House then took up the report of the Committee of the Whole clause by clause. A two-thirds vote was necessary for adoption by the House. When the House came to the first proposal on religion, Fisher Ames of Massachusetts proposed a new wording as follows:

Congress shall make no law establishing religion, or to prevent the free exercise thereof, or to infringe the rights of conscience.[23]

This motion was then adopted by the House and the section limiting the powers of the states was also adopted by the House by at least two-thirds vote. (The exact record of voting is not given in the *Annals*.) Both of Madison's major proposals on religion were thus victorious in the House of Representatives on August 20, 1789.

The official wording of the entire set of seventeen proposed amendments as agreed upon by the House is stated in the *Journal of the House of Representatives* for August 21, 1789. The third article read as follows:

Congress shall make no law establishing religion, or prohibiting the free exercise thereof, nor shall the rights of conscience be infringed.[24]

The fourth article made a similar limitation upon Congress with respect to freedom of speech, press, assembly, and petition. The eleventh article read as follows:

No state shall infringe the right of trial by jury in criminal cases; nor the rights of conscience; nor the freedom of speech or of the press.[25]

On August 22 the House finished its approval of the whole set of amendments and they were referred to a committee to arrange the amendments and report to the House. On August 24 the committee's report was accepted, and the amendments were ordered to be sent to the Senate with a request for concurrence. This committee had changed the number of the eleventh article and made it into the fourteenth, but no changes were made in the content. This was the order in which the list was sent to the Senate, incorporating all of Madison's basic ideas concerning civil rights and liberties.

Since the debates in the Senate are not available in as much detail as those in the House, it is difficult to follow the arguments or the specific reasons for the Senate's actions. However, the basic record is clear. The *Senate Journal* records the fact that on August 24 the House proposals for seventeen amendments to the Constitution were received.[26] It was immediately moved to postpone consideration of these proposals until the next session of Congress, but the motion was defeated.

The Senate began debate on the proposed amendments on September 3, 1789. On that day several changes in the wording of the third article were proposed, indicating that the meanings of the words were important. The first motion was to amend article three by striking out the inclusive word "religion" and inserting "One Religious Sect or Society in preference to others."[27] This would have made the article read:

Congress shall make no law establishing one Religious Sect or Society in preference to others, or prohibiting the free exercise thereof, nor shall the rights of conscience be infringed.

This version was obviously intended to try to do away with the broad limitation of the House's wording and reduce the limitation simply to prohibiting a single national church in preference to others. This was exactly the meaning of single establishment and would have allowed multiple establishment. Apparently some groups in the Senate wished to confine the powers of Congress to this earlier meaning of establishment. But the Senate defeated this motion, apparently preferring to prohibit the broader meaning of multiple establishment which was clearly in the House wording.

It was then moved to strike out article three altogether, but this motion was defeated. Then a motion was made to substitute a new article in place of the House proposal as follows:

> Congress shall make no law establishing any particular denomination of religion in preference to another, or prohibiting the free exercise thereof, nor shall the rights of conscience be infringed.[28]

Here was a second attempt to change the meaning of the House proposal and narrow the prohibition from multiple establishment to single establishment. This wording would have allowed multiple establishment, but it was defeated. Then a motion was made to adopt the House proposal as it stood, but this too was defeated. Finally, a motion was made to adopt the first two clauses of the House proposal as they stood but to strike out the last clause, "nor shall the rights of conscience be infringed."[29] This motion was passed. Thus, in these debates the Senate was apparently willing to accept the prohibition upon multiple establishment but was not willing to go so far as to exempt in so many words the rights of conscience from Congressional action. It may be that the Senate was afraid to give the same rights to non-believers as to believers.

On September 7, 1789 the Senate again showed its reluctance to grant equal rights of conscience to all and showed that it was unwilling to put these limitations upon the states. It defeated the motion to adopt the fourteenth article as proposed by the House and thus failed to take the step which Congress finally took when it passed the Fourteenth Amendment as adopted by the states in 1868. It took eighty years of history and the Civil War to bring the federal government to the place where it would limit the states in their freedom to infringe the civil liberties of all its citizens. Many trials and much tribulation could have been saved in the march toward democracy if the Senate had concurred with the House on its fourteenth article in 1789. Madison's foresight and intentions were never clearer than on this issue.

On September 7, 8, and 9, 1789 the Senate continued its consideration of the proposed amendments received from the House. In the course of its debates the Senate made many counter proposals and defeated a large number of proposals for additions to the list. On September 9 the Senate came back to article three, and it was again amended, this time to try once more to weaken the broad House prohibition upon multiple establishment. The following wording was adopted:

Congress shall make no law establishing articles of faith or a mode of worship, or prohibiting the free exercise of religion . . . .[30]

This version was limited to free exercise of worship in both its clauses and would have allowed financial support for one or more churches just so long as the government gave no legal sanction to any one kind of belief or form of worship in preference to others. At this time the fourth article was dropped, but its content concerning freedom of speech, press, assembly, and petition was incorporated into the third article. As a result of its actions, the Senate reduced the House list from seventeen to twelve proposed amendments and also submitted twenty-six counter proposals for changes in the House amendments, including the one on religion. It was then ordered on September 9 that the whole set of resolutions be taken back to the House; this was done on September 10.

On September 21 the House took up the Senate's proposals, agreed to ten of the Senate's counter proposals but disagreed with sixteen of them. The House thereupon notified the Senate of its agreements and asked for a conference committee to be appointed to work on the disagreements. The House appointed Madison, Roger Sherman of Connecticut, and John Vining of Delaware to the conference committee.[31] The Senate voted to recede from only one of its proposals and agreed to a conference committee to which it appointed Oliver Ellsworth of Connecticut, Charles Carroll of Maryland, and William Paterson of New Jersey.[32] On September 23 Madison reported the deliberations of the conference committee to the House,[33] and on September 24 Ellsworth reported to the Senate.[34] Ellsworth's report showed clearly that the conference managers of the House, led by Madison, were willing to accede to all of the counter proposals of the Senate except two. These were the items closest to Madison's heart, the principle of establishment at stake in the article on religion and the article on trial by jury. Madison had won the principle of freedom of speech, press, assembly, and petition, and he was determined not to lose ground on his other two most highly prized civil rights for which he had fought since his speech of June 8. The wording for the third article, upon which the conference committee agreed and upon which Ellsworth reported that the House would insist, is the final wording of the First Amendment as eventually adopted:

> Congress shall make no LAW RESPECTING AN ESTABLISHMENT OF RELIGION, or prohibiting the free exercise thereof; or abridging the freedom of Speech, or of the Press; or the right of the People peaceably to assemble and petition the Government for a redress of Grievances.[35]

On September 24 the House approved Madison's version, and on September 25 the Senate, under pressure from the House, concurred.[36] The final version was definitely a victory for Madison and for the more democratic House. It incorporated a prohibition upon the broader meaning of "establishment" for which Madison had fought consistently ever since the time of the Virginia Declaration of Rights in 1776 and the *Remonstrance* of 1785. This detailed step-by-step evolution of the wording of the First Amendment is necessary to show that it was not accidentally or carelessly formulated. It had a definite meaning that not only stood firm against the half measures of the earlier debates in the House and final Senate version but also incorporated them into its broader meaning. The clause "an establishment of religion" included all the desires to prohibit a single established church, but it also applied to plural support of many or all religions. It not only prohibited legal sanction for any one or all doctrines or forms of worship, but also it prohibited any financial support, directly through tax funds or indirectly through land, for any one or many churches, or for religion in general.

Although the final wording does not mention specifically the equal rights of conscience, and to this extent Madison bowed to the process of group deliberation, it does incorporate the basic principle of separation of church and state which was developing in the several states. Madison also lost to the extent that the United States Constitution did not in its original Bill of Rights apply the principle of separation directly to the states. The Fourteenth Amendment of 1868 was thus made necessary to achieve this purpose. The First Amendment did, however, commit the federal government to the principle of separation as it was being defined in the majority of the states.[37] This meant not only free exercise of religious worship based upon civil rights of conscience but also the prohibition of "co-operation" by the federal government with one or with many churches. "Co-operation" of church and state is just as inimical to the equal rights of conscience as free exercise is necessary to them. The generic term "religious freedom" requires "no establishment" as fully as it requires "free exercise." A violation of either is an attack upon religious freedom.

AFTER THE FIRST AMENDMENT

Despite the fact that America was in one sense a Christian nation by virtue of majority opinion, the First Amendment meant that the government was to take no active part in promoting, sponsoring, or supporting Christianity. This principle was reaffirmed under the presidency of George Washington in a treaty negotiated with Tripoli in 1796. It states:

As the government of the United States of America is not in any sense founded on the Christian religion — as it has in itself no character of enmity against the laws, religion or tranquillity of Musselmen . . . it is declared by the parties, that no pretext arising from religious opinions shall ever produce an interruption of the harmony existing between the two countries.[38]

Inasmuch as the Constitution states that treaties have the force of the supreme law of the land, this statement is as much a principle of constitutional law as if it were contained in the Constitution itself.

That Jefferson was a prime supporter of separation of church and state during his presidency is too well known to need any other substantiation than his now famous statement contained in a letter to the Danbury (Conn.) Baptist Association made on January 1, 1802, while he was president of the United States.

Believing with you that religion is a matter which lies solely between man and his God, that he owes account to none other for his faith or his worship, that the legislative powers of government reach actions only, and not opinions, I contemplate with sovereign reverence that act of the whole American people which declared that their legislature should "make no law respecting an establishment of religion, or prohibiting the free exercise thereof," thus building a wall of separation between church and state. Adhering to this expression of the supreme will of the nation in behalf of the rights of conscience, I shall see with sincere satisfaction the progress of those sentiments which tend to restore to man all his natural rights, convinced he has no natural right in opposition to his social duties.[39]

There can be no doubt from a thorough study of the historical evidence that this statement by Jefferson is in direct line with the principles he and Madison had been espousing since 1776, from the Declaration of Independence, the Declaration of Rights of the Virginia Constitution, and the Virginia Statute for Religious Freedom to the First Amendment of the United States Constitution. His words "a wall of separation between church and state" are not simply a metaphor of one private citizen's language; they reflect accurately the intent of those most responsible for the First Amendment; and they came to reflect the majority will of the American people. The words "separation of church and state" are an accurate and convenient shorthand meaning of the First Amendment itself; they represent a well-defined historical principle from the pen of one who in many official statements and actions helped to frame the authentic American tradition of political and religious liberty.

Much effort has recently been expended to belittle Jefferson's phrase "a wall of separation between church and state" as simply a colorful metaphor contained in a little letter of courtesy which Jefferson wrote in reply to an address of felicitation from the Danbury Baptists. Jefferson, however, was not in the habit of treating lightly a subject upon which he had felt so strongly for many years. Especially was the question of religious freedom a matter of the greatest concern to Jefferson so soon after the bitter religious denunciations of him that had marked the recent presidential campaign.

The special care with which Jefferson framed this particular letter to the Danbury Baptists is attested by a letter he wrote to Levi Lincoln, his attorney general, asking for advice concerning the points made in his letter to the Baptists. Here is indisputable evidence that Jefferson had worded *this* letter with meticulous care in order to emphasize and describe a political and constitutional *principle* which he deeply believed to be of first importance. He was not idly coining a phrase for pleasure nor hurriedly dictating a formal letter of courtesy in the midst of the pressures of more important business. The letter to the attorney general, dated the same day as his letter to the Baptists, follows:

Averse to receive addresses, yet unable to prevent them, I have generally endeavored to turn them to some account, by making them the occasion, by way of answer, of *sowing useful truths & principles among the people, which might germinate and become rooted among their political tenets.* The Baptist address, now enclosed, admits of a condemnation of the alliance between Church & State, under the authority of the Constitution. It furnishes an occasion, too, which I have long wished to find, of saying why I do not proclaim fastings and thanksgivings, as my predecessors did.

The address, to be sure, does not point at this, and its introduction is awkward. But I foresee no opportunity of doing it more pertinently. I know it will give great offense to the New England clergy; but the advocate of religious freedom is to expect neither peace nor forgiveness from them. Will you be so good as to examine the answer, and suggest any alterations which might prevent an ill effect, or promote a good one among the people? You understand the temper of those in the North, and can weaken it, therefore, to their stomachs; it is at present seasoned to the Southern taste only. I would ask the favor of you to return it, with the address, in the course of the day or evening.[40]

So broadly did Jefferson understand the First Amendment to apply to the separation of church and state that he consistently refused, as chief executive, to issue proclamations concerning religious fasts or thanksgivings. He felt that such proclamations would commit the executive and thereby the government to promoting religious activities and might be construed as an infringement of the free exercise of religion. He defended his position on this matter in his second inaugural as follows:

In matters of religion, I have considered that its free exercise is placed by the constitution independent of the powers of the general government — I have therefore undertaken, on no occasion, to prescribe the religious exercises suited to it; but have left them as the constitution found them, under the direction and discipline of state or church authorities acknowledged by the several religious societies.[41]

This phrasing was formulated with Madison's advice as a defense for Jefferson's keeping strictly hands off the free exercise of religion. This reflected Jefferson's concern to keep the federal government neutral in matters of religion so that it could not be charged with promoting religion in any respect, even to the impartial promotion of religion. The statement recognized, too, that the federal government did not have the power under the Constitution to decide for the states what their attitudes toward religious proclamations should be, but Jefferson's whole history in Virginia showed clearly that he thought the attitude of the states should be the same as that of the federal government. Both should be neutral.

Jefferson later elaborated on this point in a letter of January 23, 1808 to Reverend Samuel Miller in which he stated that he had refused to give political sanction to religious exercises on the grounds that the First Amendment had prohibited such authority to the federal government and reserved it to the states, "as far as it can be in any human authority." He realized that state governors had long issued such proclamation and that Washington and Adams had done so as president, but he felt that the president should not presume to exert *even indirect* authority or guidance over religious exercises. In those states whose constitutions did not fully protect religious freedom, the governor "might" have a right to issue proclamations, but in states where the people were protected by a bill of rights as they were by the First Amendment, there would be no such right:

Every religious society has a right to determine for itself the times for these exercises, and the objects proper for them, according to their particular tenets; and this right can never be safer than in their own hands where the constitution has deposited it.[42]

The whole tenor of this and other letters re-enforced Jefferson's position that the powers of the government are entirely civil and are completely shorn of *any* authority to "co-operate" with some religious groups or with all of them or even in so indirect a way as simply to *recommend* a day of fasting and prayer. The Constitution did not leave religious rights under the power of any public functionary.[43]

Madison, during his two terms as president, was fully as strict as Jefferson in his application of the principle of separation to specific actions. On February 21, 1811, Madison vetoed a bill to incorporate the Episcopal Church of Alexandria, then in the District of Columbia. He there stated:

> . . . the bill exceeds the rightful authority to which governments are limited by the essential distinction between civil and religious functions, and violates in particular the article of the Constitution of the United States which declares that "Congress shall make no law respecting a religious establishment . . . ." This particular church, therefore, would so far be a religious establishment by law, a legal force and sanction being given to certain articles in its constitution and administration.[44]

On February 28, 1811 Madison vetoed a bill to reserve certain public lands for a Baptist Church in the Mississippi Territory:

> *Because* the bill in reserving a certain parcel of land of the United States for the use of said Baptist Church comprises a *principle* and a precedent for the appropriation of funds of the United States for the use and *support* of *religious societies,* contrary to the article of the Constitution which declares that "Congress shall make no law respecting a religious establishment."[45]

These vetoes show a direct continuity in Madison's thinking from the Virginia Declaration of Rights, his *Memorial* and

Remonstrance against Religious Assessment, and the Virginia Statute for Religious Freedom to the First Amendment. *He thought of establishment as any kind of legal support or financial support for any church. He did not think of establishment as simply the establishment of a single national church.*

Upon his retirement from the presidency Madison elaborated in still more detail his views of the application of the principle of separation to other aspects of the relation between church and state. He stated clearly that he believed all of the following were examples of "an establishment of religion": tax exemption for churches, chaplains for Congress when paid by public funds, chaplains for the army and navy when paid by public funds, and religious proclamations by the chief executive.

In papers which Madison wrote a few years after his retirement he elaborated his views on the above subjects and indicated clearly that the problem of separation of church and state was one of his most cherished concerns from his first days as one of the youngest members of the Virginia Constitutional Convention to his latter days as an elder statesman. Excerpts from these papers illustrate his points and show unmistakably that when he said *separation* (and he used the word often) he meant separation in an even more thoroughgoing sense than has yet been fully achieved in American practice:

Strongly guarded as is the *separation between Religion & Govt in the Constitution of the United States* the danger of encroachment by Ecclesiastical Bodies, may be illustrated by precedents already furnished in their short history. (See the cases in which negatives were put by J. M. on two bills passd by Congs and his signature withheld from another. See also attempt in Kentucky for example, where it was proposed to exempt Houses of Worship from taxes.[46]

On the subject of chaplains in Congress and in the army and navy Madison showed that he interpreted "establishment of religion" to include payment of salaries to chaplains (with public funds) even if they were selected fairly and impartially among all religious sects; he states plainly that the *principle* of establishment violates the principle of religious freedom:

Is the appointment of Chaplains to the two Houses of Congress consistent with the Constitution, and with the *pure principle of religious freedom?*

In strictness the answers on both points must be in the negative. The Constitution of the U. S. *forbids everything like an establishment of a national religion.* The law appointing Chaplains establishes a religious worship for the national representatives, to be performed by Ministers of religion, elected by a majority of them; and these are to be paid out of the national taxes. Does not this involve the *principle of a national establishment,* applicable to a provision for a religious worship for the Constituent as well as of the representative Body, approved by the majority, and conducted by Ministers of religion paid by the entire nation.

The establishment of the chaplainship to Congs is a palpable violation of equal rights, as well as of Constitutional principles: The tenets of the chaplains elected (by the majority) shut the door of worship agst the members whose creeds & consciences forbid a participation in that of the majority. To say nothing of other sects, this is the case with that of Roman Catholics & Quakers who have always had members in one or both of the Legislative branches. Could a Catholic clergyman ever hope to be appointed a Chaplain? To say that his religious principles are obnoxious or that his sect is small, is to lift the evil at once and exhibit in its naked deformity the doctrine that religious truth is to be tested by numbers, or that the major sects have a right to govern the minor.

If Religion consist in voluntary acts of individuals, singly, or voluntarily associated, and it be proper that public functionaries, as well as their Constituents shd discharge their religious duties, let them like their Constituents, *do so at their own expence.* How small a contribution from each member of Congs wd suffice for the purpose? How just wd it be in its principle? How noble in its exemplary sacrifice to the genius of the Constitution; and the divine right of conscience? Why should the expence of a religious worship be allowed for the Legislature, be paid by the public, more than that for the Ex. or Judiciary branch of the Govt. . . .

Better also to disarm in the same way, the precedent of Chaplainships for the army and navy, than erect them into a political authority in matter of religion. The object of this *establishment* is seducing; the motive to it is laudable. But is it not safer to adhere to a right *principle,* and trust to its consequences, than confide in the reasoning however specious in favor of a wrong one.[47]

On the subject of religious proclamations Madison said:

Religious proclamations by the Executive recommending thanksgiving & fasts are shoots from the same root with the legislative acts reviewed.

Altho' recommendations only, they imply a religious agency, making no part of the trust delegated to political rulers.

The objections to them are . . . 3. They seem to imply and certainly nourish the erronious idea of a *national* religion. The idea just as it related to the Jewish nation under a theocracy, having been improperly adopted by so many nations which have embraced Xnity, is too apt to lurk in the bosoms even of Americans, who in general are aware of the distinction between religious & political societies. The idea also of a union of all to form one nation under one Govt in acts of devotion to the God of all is an imposing idea. But reason and the principles of the Xn religion require that all the individuals composing a nation even of the same precise creed & wished to unite in a universal act of religion at the same time, the union ought to be effected thro' the intervention of their religious not of their political representatives. In a nation composed of various sects, some alienated widely from others, and where no agreement could take place thro' the former, the interposition of the latter is doubly wrong: . . .5. The last & not the least objection is the liability of the practice to a subserviency to political views; to the scandal of religion, as well as the increase of party animosities. Candid or incautious politicians will not always disown such views. In truth it is difficult to frame such a religious Proclamation generally suggested by a political State of things, without referring to them in terms having some bearing on party questions.[48]

Following up these sketchy notes in the *Memoranda,* Madison wrote an excellent and carefully drawn statement of his mature views on separation of church and state in a letter to

Edward Livingston on July 10, 1822. The ideas are obviously the same as those in the *Memoranda*:

I observe with particular pleasure the view you have taken of the immunity of Religion from civil jurisdiction, in every case where it does not trespass on private rights or the public peace. *This has always been a favorite principle with me;* and *it was not with my approbation, that the deviation from it took place in Congress, when they appointed Chaplains, to be paid from the National Treasury.* [Italics added] It would have been a much better proof to their constituents of their pious feeling if the members had contributed for the purpose, a pittance from their own pockets. As the precedent is not likely to be rescinded, the best that can now be done, may be to apply to the Constitution the maxim of the law, de minimis non curat.

There has been another deviation from the *strict principle* [italics added] in the Executive Proclamations of fasts and festivals, so far, at least, as they have spoken the language of *injunction,* or have lost sight of the equality of *all* religious sects in the eye of the Constitution. Whilst I was honored with the Executive Trust I found it necessary on more than one occasion to follow the example of predecessors. But I was always careful to make the Proclamations absolutely indiscriminate, and merely recommendatory; or rather mere *designations* of a day, on which all who thought proper might *unite* in consecrating it to religious purposes, according to their own faith and forms. In this sense, I presume you reserve to the Government a right to *appoint* particular days for religious worship throughout the State, without any penal sanction enforcing the worship. I know not what may be the way of thinking on this subject in Louisiana. I should suppose the Catholic portion of the people, at least, as a small and even unpopular sect in the United States, would rally, as they did in Virginia when religious liberty was a legislative topic, to its broadest principle. Notwithstanding the general progress made within the two last centuries in favor of this branch of liberty, and the full establishment of it, in some parts of our Country, there remains in others a strong bias towards the old error, that without some sort of alliance or coalition between Government and Religion neither can be duly supported. Such indeed is the tendency to such a coalition, and such its corrupting influence on both the parties, that the danger cannot be too carefully guarded against. And in a

Government of opinion, like ours, the only effectual guard must be found in the soundness and stability of the general opinion on the subject. Every new and successful example therefore of *a perfect separation between ecclesiastical and civil matters* [italics added] is of importance. And I have no doubt that every new example, will succeed, as every past one has done, in showing that religion and Government will both exist in greater purity, *the less they are mixed together* [italics added]. It was the belief of all sects at one time that the establishment of Religion by law, was right and necessary; that the true religion ought to be established in exclusion of every other; and that the only question to be decided was which was the true religion. The example of Holland proved that a toleration of sects, dissenting from the established sect, was safe and even useful. The example of the Colonies, now States, which rejected religious establishments altogether, proved that all Sects might be safely and advantageously put on a footing of equal and entire freedom; and a continuance of their example since the declaration of Independence, has shown that its success in Colonies was not to be ascribed to their connection with the parent Country. If a further confirmation of the truth could be wanted, it is to be found in the examples furnished by the States, which have abolished their religious establishments. I cannot speak particularly of any of the cases excepting that of Virginia, where it is impossible to deny that Religion prevails with more zeal, and a more exemplary priesthood than it ever did when established and patronized by Public authority. We are teaching the world the great truth that Governments do better without Kings and Nobles than with them. The merit will be doubled by the other lesson that *Religion flourishes in greater purity, without than with the aid of Government*. [Italics added] [49]

Here, then, is substantial testimony to the principle of separation of church and state in the work and writings of Jefferson and Madison, the founding fathers whose lives spanned the launching of the new nation and whose allegiance to religious freedom and opposition to all forms of religious establishment never swerved. That their ideas were not immediately and fully put everywhere into practice is simply a result of the variety and diversity that has generally characterized so much of American life. Again, however, the trend is unmistakable.

As new states were admitted to the Union throughout the nineteenth century, their constitutions reflected the principle of separation largely as defined in the First Amendment. Despite differences in wording the common characteristics of the religious provisions show the intent to protect freedom and equality of religious conscience by assuring free exercise of religion to all orderly religious groups and by prohibiting public taxation for the support of religious groups. Thomas M. Cooley, eminent authority on constitutional law, summarizes those things that are not lawful under any of the American constitutions: no law may be passed respecting an establishment of religion, compulsory support, by taxation or otherwise, of religious instruction, compulsory attendance upon religious worship, restraints upon the expression of religious belief.[50]

The states added to the Union in the early nineteenth century reflected these principles in various ways in their constitutions. The Illinois Constitution of 1818 contains provisions that are typical of the provisions in many other state constitutions of the first half of the nineteenth century:

That all men have a natural and indefeasible right to worship Almighty God according to the dictates of their own consciences; that *no man can of right be compelled to attend, erect, or support any place of worship, or to maintain any ministry against his consent;* that no human authority can, in any case whatever, control or interfere with the rights of conscience; and that *no preference shall ever be given by law to any religious establishments or modes of worship.*[51]

The italicized words show clearly the intent to prevent the use of public funds for *any* religious group, an intent directly in line with the meaning of the "establishment of religion" clause of the First Amendment. The final clause shows clearly by the use of plurals in the words "religious establishments or modes of worship" that multiple co-operation between the state and a large number of churches is just as much prohibited as is co-operation between the state and a single church.

A careful inspection of all state constitutions will show that every original state constitution outside of the Eastern seaboard (except possibly Louisiana and Mississippi) contains a similar prohibition against compulsory support of *any* place of worship or maintenance of *any* ministry of religion. In most cases the actual wording is repeated or parallels the form contained in the constitutions of Pennsylvania, New Jersey, and North Carolina (all framed in 1776) and in the Virginia Statute for Religious Freedom of 1786. The intention in all these provisions is clearly to prohibit "an establishment of religion." The state constitutions as well as the First Amendment were all intended to prohibit multiple establishment as well as single establishment. They are all part of the same historical process.

Several state constitutions in addition to those of Illinois in 1818 and Wisconsin in 1848 use the words in the plural, "religious establishments or modes of worship." The Michigan Constitution of 1837 spells out the prohibition by adding the words "No money shall be drawn from the treasury for the benefit of religious societies, or theological or religious seminaries." The constitutions of Iowa, Utah, South Carolina, and Louisiana use the exact words of the First Amendment. Space will not permit further examples from the state constitutions, but the main lines of the historic principle of separation of church and state are as clear with respect to prohibition of support of religion (meaning no single or multiple establishment) as they are with respect to the free exercise of religion.

A thoroughgoing study of all state constitutions here is obviously impossible, but the actual provisions may be studied in such a compilation as that of C. H. Moehlman, *American Constitutions and Religion* (Berne, Indiana, 1938) or in such a standard work as that of Thorpe cited above. From 1876 onward all new states added to the Union were required by Congress to include in their basic laws an irrevocable ordinance guaranteeing religious freedom in line with the principles of the First Amendment.[52]

THE FOURTEENTH AMENDMENT

The final step in the application of the basic principle of separation on the national level began with the adoption of the Fourteenth Amendment to the Constitution in July, 1868. The first section of the Fourteenth Amendment reads as follows:

All persons born or naturalized in the United States, and subject to the jurisdiction thereof, are citizens of the United States and of the State wherein they reside. No State shall make or enforce any law which shall abridge the privileges or immunities of citizens of the United States; nor shall any State deprive any person of life, liberty, or property, without due process of law; nor deny to any person within its jurisdiction the equal protection of the laws.

Thus was achieved through constitutional amendment those limitations upon the states with respect to civil rights which the Bill of Rights of the Constitution imposes on the federal government itself. Thus was brought to fruition the efforts that Madison and the House of Representatives made in the First Congress to prohibit the states from infringing such civil rights as the equal rights of conscience, freedom of the press, and trial by jury. The Fourteenth Amendment was in direct line with the principles of the makers of the original Bill of Rights contained in the first ten amendments.

The Fourteenth Amendment was one of the three amendments (along with the Thirteenth prohibiting slavery and the Fifteenth prohibiting special qualifications for voting) which were passed in the reconstruction period following the Civil War. These were the only three amendments that put limitations upon the powers of the states up to that time. As early as 1896, it was widely accepted that the Fourteenth Amendment applied to the states the same protection of individual rights and liberties that had been applied to the federal government by the original Bill of Rights. Referring to these three amendments, an eminent historian stated in 1896:

Already the individual was amply protected from the tyranny of the central power, now the sphere of individual liberty was extended by the imposition of restrictions upon state aggression. Except for the power of enforcement, no additional power is given to the United States by the "reconstruction amendments." They are in terms a subtraction from the powers of the States and the United States, but in effect "the position of the United States is changed from that of a passive noninfringer of individual liberty to that of an active defender of the same against the State."[53]

Prior to the Fourteenth Amendment the Supreme Court had been struggling with the problem raised by the fact that the Bill of Rights not only guaranteed individual liberties but also guaranteed that no person shall be "deprived of life, liberty, or property without *due process of law*" (Fifth Amendment). During a large part of the nineteenth century the Supreme Court tended to identify liberty with property as defined by John Marshall and Joseph Story, and when liberty and property came into conflict, property was likely to come off the winner. Thus, government was interpreted as not being able to deprive any person of property that he had already acquired. The doctrine of vested rights as defined by Marshall and Story culminated in the Dred Scott decision and ultimately came to mean virtually that government had no right even by "due process of law" to interfere with property rights even though they infringed upon the civil liberties of other people.

However, in the twentieth century the Supreme Court began to emphasize the Fourteenth Amendment as a protection of the civil rights and liberties of individuals and minority groups even against property rights when necessary. As early as 1925 in the Gitlow case the Supreme Court used the Fourteenth Amendment to protect individuals from infringement of their civil rights by the states:

> For present purposes we may and do assume that freedom of speech and of the press — which are protected by the First Amendment from abridgement by Congress — are among the fundamental personal rights and "liberties" protected by the due process clause of the Fourteenth Amendment from impairment by the States.[54]

Thus began the process by which the various aspects of the First Amendment were made applicable to the states by the Fourteenth Amendment. A whole series of cases bearing on freedom of speech, press, assembly, and petition was decided in the 1930's. During the 1940's the Supreme Court made the free-exercise clause of the First Amendment applicable to the states through the Fourteenth Amendment.[55] In 1947 the Supreme Court decision in the Everson case took the next logical step and gave the same interpretation to the "establishment of religion" clause of the First Amendment and made it applicable to the states through the Fourteenth Amendment. In the Everson case the Supreme Court majority stated the principle (with which the minority agreed) as follows:

> The "establishment of religion" clause of the First Amendment means at least this: Neither a state nor the Federal Government can set up a church. *Neither can pass laws which aid one religion, aid all religions, or prefer one religion over another.* Neither can force nor influence a person to go to or to remain away from church against his will or force him to profess a belief or disbelief in any religion. No person can be punished for entertaining or professing religious beliefs or disbeliefs, for church attendance or non-attendance. *No tax in any amount, large or small, can be levied to support any religious activities or institutions, whatever they may be called, or whatever form they may adopt to teach or practice religion.* Neither a state nor the Federal Government can, openly or secretly, participate in the affairs of any religious organizations or groups and *vice versa.* In the words of Jefferson, the

clause against establishment of religion by law was intended to erect "a wall of separation between Church and State."[56]

No clearer statement could be made to show that the principle of separation of church and state as defined in the Everson case is in direct line with the historic meaning of the separation of church and state in America. In general, the process whereby the principle of complete "co-operation" of church and state has been replaced by the principle of complete separation of church and state has involved four historical steps:

(1) *Revolutionary and Early National Period*
In order to protect the civil rights of the citizens of the several states, the bills of rights of most of the early state constitutions separated church from state by prohibiting the states from making single or multiple establishments of religion.

(2) *Early National Period*
In order to protect the civil rights of the citizen of the United States, the First Amendment of the Constitution separated church from state by prohibiting the federal government from making single or multiple establishments of religion. The states followed suit in their own constitutions.

(3) *Reconstruction Period*
In order to protect the civil rights of citizens of the United States from infringement by the several states, the Fourteenth Amendment made the First Amendment applicable to the states and thus prohibited the states from infringing the equal rights of conscience and freedom of speech, press, assembly, and petition as defined by the First Amendment. The Supreme Court so interpreted the meaning of the Fourteenth Amendment when cases began to come to it in the twentieth century.

(4) *Late Nineteenth Century to the Present*

The Supreme Court gradually brought its decisions of the last fifty years into line with the intent of Madison and the framers of the First and Fourteenth Amendments. In order to protect the civil rights of all American citizens, the federal government has the right to enforce separation of church and state upon the several states by prohibiting single or multiple establishments of religion in the states. As indicated throughout this study, "establishment of religion" has always implied legal and financial support for religion. State support for one or for many religions, whether preferentially or impartially, is thus prohibited. Far from being a perversion of the original meaning of separation, the principle enunciated in the Everson case is the logical culmination of the authentic historical tradition of the principle of separation of church and state as it has developed from 1776 to the present time.[57]

Despite the clarity of the principle of separation of church and state as expressed in this authentic historical tradition, there have been many practices continued which are in effect holdovers from the pre-separation days of the seventeenth and eighteenth centuries. These practices include religious phraseology in several state constitutions, the appointment and payment of chaplains for Congress, for the armed forces, and for certain penal and charitable institutions, tax exemptions for religious institutions, religious exercises at official ceremonies, and certain requirements for religious oaths and tests for officeholders of a few state governments. The weight of evidence indicates that these practices are exceptions to the principle of separation of church and state rather than practices which prove the principle of "co-operation" between church and state. The principle is clearly "separation" and not "co-operation."

The historical experience indicates that renewed efforts to expand and enlarge such practices of "co-operation" might bring about a reaction among the American people that would lead them to turn upon these remaining practices in the effort to take away the advantages of public support where they exist. Such practices have been justified because of their contributions to the public welfare, but, as in the days of the assessment battles in Virginia, if the people are forced to choose between expanded or multiple religious establishments at public expense and the preservation of the public peace and welfare, they are likely to choose the latter, as they have done so often in the past. Such a decision would in no sense arise from an anti-religious feeling or from a hostility toward any religion. It would simply mean an adherence to the principle of separation whereby religious matters are the concern of the individual and of religious agencies, but not of the civil government.

The boundary lines between secular and religious affairs are, of course, very difficult to determine, and that is why the struggle for separation of church and state in practice seems to be a never-ending struggle. Religious and civil matters run into each other in many ways. Court decisions affect churches; the government's right of eminent domain applies to church properties as to all other properties; and political efforts of religious groups to influence social legislation make it difficult to keep religion and politics in watertight compartments. This latter has been true from the days of slavery, prohibition, Sunday observance, and child labor up to present problems of conscientious objectors, divorce, and birth control. Of such difficult problems, however, the most difficult of all is the problem of education.

In education, as elsewhere, decisions should take into account the clearest and best evidence with respect to the historic meaning of separation of church and state. Here, above all, should decisions of public policy be made in the light of the public welfare rather than in the light of religious preferences. Here, a determination to make such decisions on the basis of the common, secular agreements of a community made up of differing religious orientations is a necessity that need not be a matter of hostility to religion in any form. It is simply a recognition of the realities of the bitter American experience with establishments of religion and the struggles involved in achieving separation of church and state. Neutrality of the state toward religion need not reflect an anti-religious attitude. Neutrality and not "co-operation" of church and state is definitely required if America is to avoid the double pitfalls of the established religions of earlier times or the attacks upon religious freedom of more recent times. Neutrality and not "co-operation" is required if America is to achieve genuine equality of religious conscience which is at the heart of our basic civil rights. Central to this task is the achievement and preservation of a common school dedicated to the avoidance of these double dangers and dedicated to the fostering of our basic democratic heritage which relies so heavily upon the values of genuine religious freedom.

5

The Meaning of Separation for Education in the Nineteenth Century

THE TRANSITION FROM private to public education in America took place in the first half of the nineteenth century after the principle of the separation of church and state had been clearly stated on both national and state levels but before it had been applied everywhere in practice. Indeed, education is one of the best examples to show how the principle itself came to be applied in practice during the early decades of the new nation. Even though the main tenets of separation had been enunciated by the beginning of the nineteenth century, the application to education came slowly in some states and more rapidly in others. Again, as was the case with the general principle of separation itself, the development of its application to education was an historical process that moved along an uneven front in various states. The process would have been speeded up and simplified if Madison had not lost his fight to make the principles of the First Amendment applicable to the states in 1789. However, the principle of separation as applied to education was well developed in most states by the Civil War, and by the turn of the twentieth century the principle of separation was widely accepted as applicable to American public education in virtually all states. There were, however, wide variations of interpretation concerning what the principle meant for practice.

During this historical process most of the difficult issues of separation in education have centered around two main problem areas, namely, the use of public funds for religious schools, and religious instruction in the public schools. In its most general form the principle of separation of church and state came to embrace these two propositions:

1. Public funds shall not be granted to religious schools.
2. Sectarian religious instruction shall not be given in the public schools.

It was a long and painful process to achieve these principles in practice. In general, the process of arriving at agreement on these two principles during the nineteenth century went through three stages somewhat similar to the stages through which the principle of separation itself went during the eighteenth century. These stages were, of course, not parallel in time, but rather the process in education tended to repeat the process through which the broader efforts at separation went. Furthermore, these stages were not clear cut, discrete, nor uniform throughout the country. At any one cross section of time in the nineteenth century, evidences of all three could be found at once. Again, however, the general trend to the end of the nineteenth century is unmistakable.

America moved away from sectarian schools designed to promote religious doctrines and worship and moved toward a common school supported by public funds, free and available to all, and designed to promote democratic citizenship. The curriculum of American schools moved away from a content permeated with religion toward a content based upon secular knowledge and morality. Despite the inadequacies of diagrammatic representation of historical generalizations, the following chart may be useful:

The Principle of Separation Applied to Education

From Establishment to Separation	*From Sectarian Schools to Secular Schools*
I. "Co-operation" between church and state with *no* religious freedom (Single establishment; no free exercise)	1. Sectarian religious public schools (public support for the established religion) 2. Dissenters' schools not permitted
II. "Co-operation" between church and state with *some* religious freedom	
A. Single establishment; free exercise	1. Sectarian religious public schools (public support for the established religion) 2. Private sectarian religious schools permitted (private support for the dissenting religions) 3. Private secular schools permitted (private support)
B. Multiple establishment; free exercise	1. Non sectarian religious public schools (public support for the Protestant religion) 2. Private sectarian religious schools permitted (private *and* public support) 3. Private secular schools permitted (private *and* public support)
III. Separation of church and state (No establishment; complete religious freedom)	1. Secular public school (public funds) 2. Private sectarian schools permitted (private support but *no* public funds) 3. Private secular schools permitted (private support but *no* public funds)

EDUCATION UNDER "CO-OPERATION" BETWEEN CHURCH AND STATE WITH NO RELIGIOUS FREEDOM

(SINGLE ESTABLISHMENT AND NO FREE EXERCISE)

In the first stage of "co-operation" between church and state (as described in Chapter 2) the schools reflected the doctrine that an establishment of religion required state support for the orthodox religion and state prohibition of all other religious beliefs (single establishment; *no* free exercise). The best educational examples of this principle are to be seen in the seventeenth century schools of Puritan New England. The early school laws of Massachusetts in 1642 and 1647, Connecticut in 1650, New Haven in 1655, Plymouth in 1677, and New Hampshire in 1680 all enunciated the principle that education was designed for the benefit of both church and state. The state required religious education in Puritan doctrine, and the state took the first steps in providing public support for public sectarian religious schools. The state made it possible for local taxes to be levied for the support of public or town schools in which instruction in established religious doctrines played a dominant role. Town support of ministers and town support of schoolmasters were parallel aspects of close "co-operation" between church and state. Religious orthodoxy was required of teachers, and dissenters' schools were considered to be as objectionable as dissenters themselves. Similar state encouragement was given to religious education in Virginia and other colonies where the Anglican church was established, but these colonies did not go so far in using the state to enforce compulsory education or to make education free to all.

EDUCATION UNDER "CO-OPERATION" BETWEEN CHURCH
AND STATE WITH SOME FREE EXERCISE OF RELIGION

Single Establishment

When the demand grew in the eighteenth century for greater
toleration and then still greater free exercise of religious worship (see Chapter 2), the educational equivalent took the
form of the development of a variety of private sectarian religious schools each supported and promoted by the voluntary
effort of the various religious denominations. Where single
establishment existed, public funds still went to support the
schools of the preferred religion. The private sectarian schools
came to be a prominent feature of the eighteenth century
scene especially in those colonies where a large number of
dissenting sects created a heterogeneous population. Schools
sponsored by Presbyterians, Dutch Reformed, Quakers, Baptists, Lutherans, German Reformed, Moravians, Mennonites,
Catholics, Methodists, Puritans, Anglicans, and other groups
made their appearance and prospered according to the efforts
of the various sects.

When the dissenter groups could freely conduct their public
worship, they began to promote their own religious schools.
The Great Awakening of the mid-eighteenth century was thus
a great promoter of sectarian education as well as a promoter
of sectarian religion in general. The increasing freedom of
schooling also made it possible for private secular schools[1] to
appear and to flourish during the early and middle part of
the eighteenth century until the academies supplanted them.
When certain sects grew strong enough they often applied for
and obtained public funds from the city or state involved.
The denominational academies of the late eighteenth century

often received such aid. When this began to happen, when public funds raised by taxation began to go to a variety of sectarian religious schools, "co-operation" between church and state in education began to move into the form of multiple establishment.

Multiple Establishment

As described in Chapter 3, the effort to maintain and extend "co-operation" between church and state was sometimes broadened during the eighteenth century to include many churches and not just one. Despite the clarity with which multiple co-operation was defined as establishment by Madison and other founding fathers, the tradition of religion in education was so strong that it seemed to many persons that freedom of religion *could* be reconciled with multiple establishment in education and that the state could properly encourage by support the religious schools of various sects. Since education was not made a function of the federal government by the Constitution, the question of separation in education on a national basis was not involved. Since, at the time of the Constitution, education was not even widely seen as a function of the state governments, the issue did not appear in the states as urgent until the period of 1820 to 1850 when state responsibility for education was proposed as the best way to develop a common school for all.

Thus the issue of separation as applied to education did not become a matter of controversy until *after* the principle of separation was decided in general and until *after* the movement for creation of a public school system was under way. When the established traditions of sectarian education were confronted with new demands for a common school, the issue of separation in education was precipitated and had to be faced.

When the educational revival of the 1820's to 1850's began

to gain momentum, the advocates of a public school system ran head on into the issue of separation. The first attempts of the public school advocates to resolve the issue and to create a common school open free to *all* and aimed at creating a democratic citizenry took the form of the non-sectarian religious public school. Horace Mann and others saw quickly that a common school supported by public taxation could *not* include the teaching of any sectarian doctrines under the principle of separation as they understood it. They, therefore, believed that the requirements of religious freedom could be maintained if the public school divorced itself from *specific sectarian religious instruction*. But they also believed that the common elements of education should include not only the basic elements of an English education (principally the three R's, history, and geography) and education for citizenship but also moral education.

It seemed obvious to them that moral education must rest upon religion, but they were faced with the fact that there were many varieties of religious belief represented among the children of a common school for all. They, therefore, came to the conclusion that moral education should be based upon the common elements of Christianity to which all Christian sects would agree or to which they would take no exception. In general, these "common elements" took two forms: namely, teaching the common moral virtues of honesty, fairness, and truth, which though apparent in the Christian virtues should, however, not be taught as sectarianism; and also reading of the Bible as containing the common elements of Christian morals but reading it with no comment in order not to introduce sectarian biases. On this basis, they felt justified to require public support of the non-sectarian, religious public school by taxation upon all citizens.

If America had remained an exclusively Protestant country, this solution might have satisfied many people, despite the clear fact that a non-sectarian public school represented a form of co-operation between the state and many religious groups, in effect, a multiple establishment of religion in education. The practical difficulty arose, however, because America became increasingly heterogeneous in religious belief. The great increases in immigration from Ireland and Germany in the period from 1820 to 1860 brought large numbers of Roman Catholics to America. When faced with the prospect of sending their children to the "non-sectarian" public school, they soon raised the objection that what seemed to be "non-sectarian" to Protestants was actually "sectarian" to Catholics.

They, therefore, objected to the sectarian quality of the public schools and made two general efforts to remedy the situation. They tried to have the Protestant "non-sectarian" instruction, including the Bible, removed from the public schools, and they tried to obtain a share of the public funds for their own parochial schools in order that their rights of conscience would not be infringed by being forced to attend a public school where Protestant teachings were presented.

It was this situation which brought about appeal to the principle of separation of church and state and made necessary its application to education. The over-all result, after years of controversy and agitation, was that the majority of Americans decided that the only possible practical decision was to follow the principles of Madison and Jefferson that true protection for equal rights of conscience requires that *all* religious instruction be eliminated from the public schools (free exercise) and that no public funds could be used for the support of religious schools (no establishment). Although specific appeal was not widely made before the Civil War to the First Amendment, because it had not yet been applied directly to the states, the results achieved by state action were in general accordance with the principle of separation as defined in the First Amendment.[2]

EDUCATION UNDER SEPARATION OF CHURCH AND STATE
(NO ESTABLISHMENT AND COMPLETE FREEDOM OF RELIGION)

Jefferson and Madison on Separation in Education

In recent years it has been maintained that the founding fathers were not opposed to "co-operation" between church and state in matters of education. It is argued, for example, that Jefferson wanted to "co-operate" with the religious sects by inviting them to establish their theological schools near the University of Virginia in order that the university students could be given religious instruction.[3]

The implication is that Jefferson would have favored impartial encouragement of all religious sects by the state. It is important, therefore, to consider briefly Jefferson's attitude toward religion in public education.

A careful study of Jefferson's entire career and his views upon education from 1779 to 1825 will show that Jefferson was one of the earliest advocates of a public education divorced from all sectarian religious influences. He saw clearly that the principle of separation of church and state for which he worked so long must mean a secular educational system.[4]

One of the sections of the revision of the laws of Virginia which Jefferson prepared and which was introduced in the Virginia legislature in 1779 was a Bill for the More General Diffusion of Knowledge. This bill for establishing a system of public elementary and secondary schools paralleled Jefferson's Bill for Religious Freedom. The education bill recognized that if no person were to be compelled to support "any religious place whatsoever," then education must be available freely to all and should contain no religious instruction. In a day when elementary instruction was highly charged with religious materials, Jefferson proposed a purely secular curriculum:

At every one of those schools shall be taught reading, writing, and common arithmetic, and the books which shall be used therein for instructing the children to read shall be such as will at the same time make them acquainted with Grecian, Roman, English, and American history.[5]

The omission of mention of religious instruction and the careful specification that reading books should be historical in nature rather than religious were Jefferson's way of ruling out religious reading materials in striking contrast to the common practice of the day. On his *Notes on Virginia* written three years later Jefferson spelled out his intention for all to see. In the section where he described the efforts to revise the whole system of laws for Virginia Jefferson had this to say about the curriculum of the elementary curriculum which he had proposed in the education bill of 1779:

Instead, therefore, of putting the Bible and Testament into the hands of the children at an age when their judgments are not sufficiently matured for religious inquiries, their memories may here be stored with the most useful facts from Grecian, Roman, European, and American history.[6]

Jefferson's proposals for secondary education in the above two documents also concentrated on the secular subjects of the Greek and Latin languages, English grammar, geography, and advanced numerical arithmetic.[7] No mention was made of religious instruction at a time when the Latin Grammar school and the religiously motivated academy were the most common types of secondary schools throughout the country.

In Jefferson's final effort to obtain passage of his cherished educational proposals he drew up a bill for public education in 1817 which embraced much of the earlier bill, but it was even more specific in its religious provisions. In the very first article Jefferson would prohibit ministers from serving as county visitors whose job was to provide for the establishment of ward schools throughout the county.[8] He thus tried to prohibit all religious control or influence in the public schools. The eleventh article effectively ruled out all religious instruction by providing that

> . . . no religious reading, instruction or exercise, shall be prescribed or practiced inconsistent with the tenets of any religious sect or denomination.[9]

For thirty-six years Jefferson was completely consistent in his view that public education should observe the principle of separation of church and state. If Virginia had been willing to accept his proposals it would have been the earliest state to establish a system of public schools in conformity with the democratic political ideals upon which the new nation was founded.

Jefferson's proposals for higher education embodied the same loyalty to the principle of separation of church and state. One of the proposals, introduced as a part of the comprehensive revisal of laws in the Virginia legislature in 1779, was a Bill for Amending the Constitution of the College of William and Mary. In this bill Jefferson was trying to reform the college of William and Mary in such a way as to bring it more into conformity with the democratic ideals and aims of a republican state. His major proposal for curriculum reform was to remove the six professors established by the original charter (two of whom were to teach theology) and to establish in their place eight professors (none of whom were to teach religion).[10] The legislature, however, did not see fit to pass this bill which would have, in effect, transformed the College of William and Mary into a state university. Jefferson attributed this failure to dissenters who were suspicious that the Anglican predispositions of the College of William and Mary might continue to color its teaching.[11]

Despite the failure of this bill to become law, Jefferson was able to achieve some of his aims while he was a member of the Board of Visitors of William and Mary in his capacity as governor. He described these moves in his *Notes on Virginia* as follows:

After the present revolution, the visitors, having no power to change those circumstances in the constitution of the college which were fixed by the charter, and being therefore confined in the number of professorships, undertook to change the objects of the professorships. They *excluded the two schools for divinity,* and that for the Greek and Latin languages, *and substituted others. . . .*[12]

After Jefferson's retirement as President of the United States he returned to Monticello and devoted much of his time to the promotion of higher education. Obliged to give up his earlier desire to transform William and Mary into a state university, he helped some of his friends promote a private academy which had been established in Albemarle County. After a canvass of European "seminaries" Jefferson put down some of his ideas in a letter of September 14, 1814 to Peter Carr who was on the board of trustees of Albemarle Academy. In this plan Jefferson proposed a modification of European universities whereby the institution should have three schools of general education devoted to languages, mathematics, and philosophy. Beyond these would be three professional schools, namely, fine arts; technical and scientific studies; and theology and law.[13]

The fact that Jefferson proposed instruction in theology for this private academy does not mean that he had departed from his loyalty to the principal of separation of church and state. A professional school of theology for "ecclesiastics" connected with a privately supported and endowed institution would be perfectly consistent with his principles. Indeed, when Jefferson soon turned to the promotion of a state university to be supported by public funds, the earlier proposals for a school of theology were conspicuous by their absence, although the other suggestions which he had made in his letter to Carr remain virtually unchanged. His Bill for the Establishment of District Colleges and University of 1817 gives full particulars concerning the branches of knowledge he would wish taught in state institutions. They were all secular, and no mention was made of religion.[14]

Finally, the legislature approved a proposal to establish a state university at Charlottesville and approved the appointment of a board of commissioners to draw up a plan for the University of Virginia. Jefferson wrote the report which was submitted to the commissioners at their meeting at Rockfish Gap in August, 1818. A careful study of this report which was adopted by the commissioners and later approved by the legislature will show that the dominant aim was to establish a state university on secular foundations. The statement of aims and the details of curriculum reflect Jefferson's social and political ideas of democracy and make no mention of religion.[15] Realizing, however, that opposition would be raised to the state university as a center of atheism because of the omission of professors of religion and theology, Jefferson included a special defense of the proposals of the commissioners in order to anticipate and mollify opposition:

In conformity with the principles of our Constitution, which places all sects of religion on an equal footing, with the jealousies of the different sects in guarding that equality from encroachment and surprise, and with the sentiments of the Legislature in favor of freedom of religion, manifested on former occasions, we have proposed no professors of divinity. . . .[16]

Instead of a professor of theology, it was proposed to leave instruction in moral philosophy to the professor of ethics and also to provide instruction in Hebrew, Greek, and Latin as depositories of the original religious writings. Summing up his position, Jefferson concluded:

Proceeding thus far without offence to the Constitution, we have thought it proper at this point to leave every sect to provide, as they think fittest, the means of further instruction in their own peculiar tenets.[17]

This was Jefferson's original intention in 1818 for keeping the University of Virginia free of religious instruction and sectarian control in conformity with the principles of religious freedom of the Constitution of Virginia. Thereupon followed long years of struggle and disappointment in the effort to obtain legislative and public support for the institution. As a result the university did not begin instruction until 1825. Gradually, the buildings were constructed and money was appropriated. As opposition from religious groups to the secular university continued with unabated vigor Jefferson found that he had to accede to demands for further recognition of the religious interests in the state.

On October 7, 1822 the minutes of the Board of Visitors of the University described a proposal made by "some pious individuals" which the Visitors accepted, but at the same time they insisted upon the principle of keeping the university independent and free of religious instruction or control. Present at this meeting of the Visitors were Jefferson as rector, Madison, James Breckenridge, Joseph C. Cabell, and John N. Cooke. The proposal was a part of the annual report of the Visitors required by law to be made to the legislature:

> The want of instruction in the various creeds of religious faith existing among our citizens presents therefore, a chasm in a general institution of the useful sciences. But it was thought that this want and the entrustment to each society of instruction in its own doctrine, were evils of less danger than a permission to the public authorities to dictate modes or principles of religious instruction, or than opportunities furnished them by giving countenance or ascendancy to any one sect over another. A remedy, however, has been suggested of promising aspect, which, while it excludes the public authorities from the domain of religious freedom, will give to the sectarian schools of divinity the full benefit the public provisions made for instruction in the other branches of science . . . . It has, therefore, been in contemplation, and suggested by some pious individuals . . . to establish their religious schools on the confines [borders] of the University, so as to give to their students

ready and convenient access and attendance on the scientific lectures of the University; . . . . Such establishments would offer the further and greater advantage of enabling the students of the University to attend religious exercises with the professor of their particular sect, either in the rooms of the building still to be erected, and destined to that purpose under impartial regulations, as proposed in the same report of the commissioners, or in the lecturing room of such professor . . . . *But always understanding that these schools shall be independent of the University and of each other.* Such an arrangement would complete the circle of useful sciences embraced by this institution, and would fill the chasm now existing, on principles which would leave inviolate the constitutional freedom of religion, the most inalienable and sound of all human rights, over which the people and authorities of this state, individually and publicly, have ever manifested the most watchful jealousy: and *could this jealousy be now alarmed, in the opinion of the legislature, by what is here suggested, the idea will be relinquished on any surmise of disapprobation which they might think proper to express.*[18]

Jefferson and Madison were willing to give somewhat unenthusiastic acceptance to this proposal in the hope that it would reconcile the religious groups to the omission of religious instruction by the university. They were willing for the students of the divinity schools to take advantage of the offerings of the university, and they were willing for university students to attend religious services given by the professors of theology. This arrangement, however, cannot be stretched to mean a "co-operation" that parallels modern programs of "released time" religious instruction. Jefferson and Madison were mindful of the constitutional principle of separation which they helped to formulate and were willing, even eager, to give up the suggestion if the legislature should have any doubts about it.

Jefferson's real feelings about the above proposal from the religious groups are best described in a frank letter to his old and close friend, Thomas Cooper, written a month later, on November 2, 1822:

In our university you know there is no Professorship of Divinity. A handle has been made of this, to disseminate an idea that this is an institution, not merely of no religion, but against all religion. Occasion was taken at the last meeting of the Visitors, to bring forward an idea that might silence this calumny which weighed on the minds of some honest friends to the institution. In our annual report to the legislature, after stating the *constitutional reasons against a public establishment of any religious instruction* we suggest the expediency of encouraging the different religious sects to establish, each for itself, a professorship of their own tenets, on the confines [boundaries or borders] of the University, so near as that their students may attend the lectures there and have the free use of our library, and every other accommodation we can give them; preserving, however, their independence of us and of each other. This fills the chasm objected to ours, as a defect in an institution professing to give instruction in *all* [italics Jefferson's] useful sciences. I think the invitation will be accepted, by some sects from candid intentions, and by others from jealousy and rivalship. And by bringing the sects together, and mixing them with the mass of other students, we shall soften their asperities, liberalize and neutralize their prejudices, and make the general religion a religion of peace, reason, and morality.[19]

"Co-operation" with the religious sects amounted to an invitation to them to build their theological schools near the grounds of the university, so that their students might take advantage of the libraries and classes which, of course, were to be open to all citizens alike. Even this much "co-operation" was a compromise designed as an "expediency" to gain the support of religious groups for the university and at the same time surrender none of the independence of the university nor permit the "public establishment of any religious instruction" in violation of the Virginia Constitution.

Jefferson's life-long devotion to "a general religion of peace, reason, and morality" did not desert him under the pressure of the sects. He was willing for them to partake equally and impartially in the services which the university could offer to the citizens of the state, but he was not willing that the university should "promote" or "aid" or "support" all religious sects equally by giving religious instruction under the auspices of the "public authorities," namely, the faculty and administration of the university.

The suggested arrangement with the religious groups was formalized by the Board of Visitors a few months prior to the opening of the first classes. This included permission for the students of the university to attend religious services at the surrounding theological schools in the mornings *before* their regular classes at the university began. The regulations adopted by the Board of Visitors on October 4, 1824 contain these provisions:

> Should the religious sects of this State, or any of them, according to the invitation held out to them, establish within, or adjacent to, the precincts of the University, schools for instruction in the religion of their sect, the students of the University will be free, and expected to attend religious worship at the establishment of their respective sects, *in the morning, and in time to meet their school in the University at its stated hour.*[20]

These same regulations prescribe exact hours for the meeting of classes at certain hours and days of the week beginning at 7:30 a.m. and ending at 3:30 p.m. Severe penalties were prescribed for absences from class, and thus if students attended religious exercises they would be obliged to be at the university in time for their first class in the morning. These regulations refer to the invitation to divinity schools to be "within, or adjacent to, the precincts of the University." The historian of the University of Virginia, however, constantly refers to the proposal as one in which the theological schools would be situated *around the boundaries* of the university or "just *without* the confines of the institution."[21] Interestingly, none of the religious sects responded immediately to the invitation "to transfer its seminary to the vicinity of the University." The Presbyterians discussed the matter in 1859 but dropped the idea in 1860.[22]

One further point should be made with respect to Jefferson's attitude toward religion at the University of Virginia. Some recent writers have been pointing out that the Board of Visitors of the university had made some provision for religious exercises to be held within university buildings. Reference can be made, for example, to the original report of the Rockfish Gap Commission in 1818 which included the following statement:

It is supposed probable, that a building of somewhat more size in the middle of the grounds may be called for in time, in which may be rooms for religious worship, under such impartial regulations as the Visitors shall prescribe, for public examination, for a library, for the schools of music, drawing, and other associated purposes.[22a]

Furthermore, the regulations of 1824 contained the following reference to the main building:

One of its larger elliptical rooms on its middle floor shall be used for annual examinations, for lectures to such schools as are too numerous for their ordinary school room, and for religious worship, under the regulations allowed to be prescribed by law.[22b]

However, it is entirely to misjudge Jefferson's intentions if these statements are interpreted to mean that Jefferson wished to use the university to promote sectarian religions impartially or in any other way. In fact the rooms mentioned were not used for such purposes. When specific proposals were made to put these provisions into practice, Jefferson's intentions and those of the Board of Visitors were made crystal clear in a letter that Jefferson wrote to A. S. Brockenbrough on April 21, 1825, in which he stated that an earlier request to hold religious services in university buildings had been refused. Jefferson further pointed out that the basis for this earlier decision was that the university buildings could only be used for university purposes. He went on to say that the original idea of using rooms on the campus for religious services had been *superseded* by the proposal that the sects establish their schools "in the vicinity" of the university. He thus rejected a second proposal to hold religious services on Sundays:

In answer to your letter proposing to permit the lecturing room of the Pavilion No. 1 to be used regularly for prayers and preachings on Sundays, I have to observe that some 3. or 4. years ago an application was made to permit a sermon to be preached in one of the pavilions on a particular occn [occasion], not now recollected, it brought the subject into considn [consideration] before the Visitors and altho' they entered into no formal and written resoln [resolution] on the occn [occasion], the concurrent sentiment was that the buildings of the Univ. belong to the state, that they were erected for the purposes of an Univ. and that the Visitors, to whose care they are commd [committed] for those purposes, have no right to permit their application to any other. . . . In the Rockfish report it was stated as probable that a building, larger than the pavilions might be called for in time, in which might be rooms for a library, for public examns [examinations] and for religious worship under such *impartial regulns [regulations] as the Visitors should prescribe.* The legislature neither sanctioned nor rejected this proposition; and afterwards, in the Report of Oct. 1822 the board suggested, as a substitute, that the difft [different] religious sects should be invited to establish their separate theological schools in the vicinity of the Univ. in which the Students might attend religious worship each in the form of his respective sect, and avoid all jealousy of attempts on his religious tenets[.] among the enactments of the board is one looking to this object, and superseding the 1st idea of permitting a room in the Rotunda to be used for religious worship, and of undertaking to frame a set of regulns [regulations] of equality and impartiality among the multiplied sects. I state these things as manifesting the caution which the board of Visitors thinks it a duty to observe on this delicate and jealous subject. your proposn [proposition] therefore leading to an applican [application] of the Univ. buildings to other than Univ. purposes, and to a partial course reguln [regulation] in favor of two particular sects, would be a deviation from the course which they think it their duty to observe.[22c]

It would be difficult to find a more thoroughgoing devotion to the idea of separation of church and state than displayed by Jefferson in his efforts to establish the University of Virginia.

To try to claim him as an advocate of increased "co-operation" between the state and the religious sects is to overlook or ignore the real meaning of those efforts as revealed by the historical record.

At a time when, in most colleges and universities of the country, ministers were presidents and commonly members of boards of control, daily chapel attendance was compulsory, courses in religion were required, and professors of theology and doctors of divinity had a prominent place on the faculties, the University of Virginia stood out sharply in contrast with its loyalty to the principle of separation of church and state. A chaplain was not appointed until 1829, and this was done after Madison, as rector following Jefferson, had written in 1828 that the support of such a chaplain should be entirely voluntary:

> I have indulged the hope that provision for religious instruction and observance among the students would be made by themselves or their parents and guardians, each contributing to a fund to be applied in remunerating the services of clergymen of denominations corresponding with the preference of the contributors. *Being altogether voluntary, it would interfere neither with the characteristic peculiarity of the University, the consecrated principle of the law, nor the spirit of the country.*[23]

Madison's concern for promoting religious exercises on a purely voluntary basis showed that he was not anti-religious but also showed his life-long meticulous concern that the civil and religious functions should not overlap. His proposal was quite in line with his earlier opposition to the payment of chaplains of Congress from public funds, but rather they should be supported by voluntary contributions (see page 98). If all public schools and public institutions of higher education in the nineteenth century had been based as firmly upon the principle of separation as was envisaged by Jefferson and Madison, much of the religious controversy in educational affairs from that time to the present might have been avoided.

Separation in Education Before the Civil War

Prior to the Civil War the trend toward separation was well under way in the states. In general, however, the movement to restrict public funds to common schools and to prevent their use for sectarian purposes gained more headway before the Civil War than did the movement to eliminate religious instruction from the public schools. Many people still thought that multiple establishment was sufficient to achieve religious freedom. Perhaps the two best examples of these trends were the states of Massachusetts and New York.

In Massachusetts the school law of 1789 provided for moral instruction based upon the general Judaeo-Christian tradition. As a means of teaching the common virtues of piety, truth, benevolence, frugality, and temperance the Bible, the Psalter, and the New Testament were widely used in the schools. However, by the time of the law of 1827 the trend toward non-sectarianism was clearly present in the provision that no books shall be used "which are calculated to favour any particular religious sect or tenet."[24] When Horace Mann began his efforts to construct a genuine state system of public schools in Massachusetts based upon the non-sectarian common elements of Christian morality, he ran into determined sectarian opposition from some of the Protestant groups who insisted that such a non-sectarian approach would make the public schools godless. They argued that morality must be based upon a sectarian religion, but Mann gradually won approval for the doctrine that morality could be based upon non-sectarian religious sanctions. The move to eliminate sectarian instruction arose from the conflicting interests among the several sectarian groups.

However, with respect to the issue of support of sectarian schools by public funds Massachusetts soon came to the principle of full separation. This culminated in a constitutional amendment of 1855 as follows:

All moneys raised by taxation in the towns and cities for the support of public schools, and all moneys which may be appropriated by the state for the support of common schools, shall be applied to, and expended in, no other schools than those which are conducted according to law, under the order and superintendence of the authorities of the town or city in which the money is to be expended; and such moneys shall never be appropriated to any religious sect for the maintenance, exclusively, of its own school.[25]

This amendment was soon applied to a statute passed by the Massachusetts legislature in 1869 which authorized the town of Andover to use public funds in support of the trustees of the Punchard Free School whose trustees were to be confined to members of the Congregational Church. A court decision held that such a school was not a public school and therefore could not receive public tax funds.[26]

At least five western states had similar constitutional provisions before the Civil War.[27] All of these constitutional provisions were so stated in direct connection with the Bill of Rights and the clauses for religious freedom as to indicate that denial of public funds for religious education was the second half of their double concern to insure free exercise of religion and to prohibit single or multiple establishments of religion.

The other outstanding controversy that led to the principle of separation in education prior to the Civil War was in New York City. Here the movement toward public support of nonsectarian Protestant religious instruction was well developed by the 1830's. In 1805 the Free School Society had been formed to educate poor children not otherwise cared for by the various sectarian denominational schools. In 1807 the Society obtained funds from the New York legislature to carry on this work which was soon expanded to serve *all* poor children free of charge. By a law of 1813 New York State divided the city's share of the state school fund among the Free School Society and three other approved philanthropic societies and "such incorporated religious societies in said city as now support or hereafter shall establish charity schools within the said city, or who may apply for the same."[28]

This was a clear example of the principle of multiple establishment. In 1820 the Bethel Baptist Church applied for and obtained a share of the public school funds to help support its school which was to be open to children of all faiths. In 1826 the Free School Society became the Public School Society and was authorized to educate *all* children, not just all poor children. The schools of the Society followed their conception of the non-sectarian ideal and based their moral instruction on the common elements of Protestant Christianity and the reading of the Bible without comment.

This was the situation, then, in the 1830's when the increasing Catholic population of New York City injected a new note. A Catholic orphan asylum applied to the city council for state funds and received them, but a Methodist charity school was denied a similar request. In 1834 Bishop Dubois complained that the school books used by the Public School Society were obviously sectarian Protestant in quality and requested that such books be submitted to him to be sure that all sectarianism and aspersions toward Catholics be omitted. The Society's trustees agreed to confer on this matter and to remove any objectionable material, but the process was never completed.[29]

The situation came to the point of real conflict in the so-called school controversy of 1840-41. The Catholics under the leadership of Bishop Hughes began a concerted campaign against the sectarianism of the Society's public schools and then precipitated the crucial struggle when they asked the city council for a share of the public school funds to support their own parochial schools. At hearings before the city council in October 1840 Bishop Hughes argued that the public schools, being Protestant, violated the rights of conscience of Catholics and that their moral instruction was based upon the common elements of *Protestant* Christianity only. He therefore concluded that the only way to insure the equal rights of conscience to Catholics was to grant them a share of the public funds.[30]

In his reply to Bishop Hughes the counsel for the Public School Society, Theodore Sedgewick, argued that the state could properly give a purely secular English education in the basic skills and a moral education based upon fundamental principles about which there was no dispute among Christians, but it could not give religious instruction based upon the specific doctrines of any of the several sects.[31] The Catholic request was turned down.[32] Here was a clear example of the quarrel over what kind of co-operation between church and state would best serve the welfare of each. The Protestants were, in general, saying that multiple establishment was acceptable to them in public common schools offering "non-sectarian" religious instruction. Catholics, however, argued that, whereas multiple establishment was also acceptable to them, it should be in the form of dividing the public funds to aid them in supporting their own Catholics schools conducted apart from the common schools.

In the following two years the Catholics carried their fight against the Public School Society to the state legislature charging that it had obtained an unfair monopoly of public school funds. In the state election of 1842 much of the campaigning was on the school issue. Catholics formed a separate political organization, endorsed several candidates already nominated, and also nominated some candidates on their own ticket for the Assembly and for the Senate. Counter-attacks were, of course, made upon the Catholics, who were charged with trying to take the Bible out of the public schools and thus making the public schools godless.

As a result of this storm of religious conflict, a law was passed by the legislature bringing New York City into the state's common school system. New York City was authorized to form a board of education and to establish a city system of ward schools alongside the schools of the Public School

Society and those of the several other approved religious or charitable agencies. This Act of 1842, however, included a provision that no public funds should go to these schools or any others if they taught sectarian religious doctrines:

No school above mentioned, or which shall be organized under this act, in which any religious sectarian doctrine or tenet shall be taught, inculcated, or practised, shall receive any portion of the school moneys to be distributed by this act . . . .[33]

As a result of the school controversy, the attempts of both Protestants and Catholics to maintain their respective versions of multiple establishment in the schools were given serious setbacks. The decision that was reached was, on the one hand, to take out of the public schools all sectarian instruction and, on the other hand, to deny public funds to sectarian schools. This, of course, did not settle the question permanently, but the logic of the situation became clear to many that complete separation was the only possible resolution of the problem of the relation of church and state in education.

Further steps were taken in this direction before the Civil War when a state law of 1848 authorizing a Catholic orphan asylum in Brooklyn to share in the public school funds was declared unconstitutional in a court decision of 1851 on the grounds that the revenue of the common school fund must be used for common schools only (article 9 of the state constitution) and that an orphanage conducted by a church was not a common school.[34]

In 1853 an important decision of the state superintendent of schools ruled that prayers could not be required as a part of the school exercises and where the King James version Bible was read in the schools, Catholic children could not be required to be present or to memorize parts of it. The arguments in this decision in the light of recent developments in New York State with respect to released time are most illuminating:

The government not relying on the ability or willingness of every part of the State to maintain efficient schools for the education of the young, by voluntary contributions, and recognizing the imperative necessity of universal education for the maintenance of our civil and political institutions, organized a general common school system. . . . The common schools were thus clearly made a government institution. To introduce into them, or permit to be introduced into them, a course of religious instruction conformable to the views of any religious denomination, would be tantamount to the adoption of a government religion — a step contrary to the Constitution, and equally at variance with the policy of a free government and the wishes of the people. *To form for the schools a course of instruction, which could bear the name of a religious one, and which would meet the views of all, was manifestly impossible. To give to every sect a pro rata share of the school moneys to enable it to support its own schools and teach its own system of religious faith in them, would be . . . to divide the children . . . into a dozen or more schools.* Indeed, under this arrangement, a single indigent family would often be required to support its own school, to go without any, or to violate its conscience by joining with others in one in which a religious system was taught wholly at variance with its own. . . .

In view of the above facts, the position was early, distinctly, and almost universally taken by our statesmen, legislators, and prominent friends of education — men of the warmest religious zeal and belonging to every sect — that *religious education must be banished from the common schools and consigned to the family and church*. . . . Accordingly, the instruction in our schools has been limited to that ordinarily included under the head of intellectual culture, and to the propagation of those principles of morality in which all sects, and *good men belonging to no sect,* can equally agree. . . . The intelligent religious public have felt that there was no tenable middle ground between thorough religious instruction in our common schools, and the broadest toleration. Driven by circumstances to adopt the latter position, they have embraced it in its most comprehensive import, and have nerved themselves to the task of supplying a lamentable omission in the public schools, by increasing assiduity to the spiritual wants of their offspring in the family circle, in the Sunday school and in the church. . . .

Not only have the Episcopalian, the Presbyterian, the Baptist and the Methodist met on *common* and *neutral* ground in the school room, but with them the Unitarian, the Universalist, the Quaker and *even the denier of all creeds. . . .*[35]

This is a remarkable statement that reveals the thinking that inevitably led to a more complete separation in education. The superintendent was obviously a deeply religious man and indeed felt that the Bible may of right be taught in the public schools, but he was firm in his belief that it should not be used to violate the conscience of Catholic children and parents. He took severe action against a teacher whose punishment of a Catholic child for refusing to memorize passages from the Bible was the occasion of the decision. Arguments like his inevitably led religious people of all faiths to the conclusion, however reluctantly, that the common school must be "common and neutral ground" with respect to religious instruction and that public funds must not be divided among the religious sects. The experiment of multiple establishment in New York was tried and found wanting. In the period following the Civil War the struggle for genuine separation took rapid strides on many fronts.

Separation in Education After the Civil War

During the last half of the nineteenth century the principle of separation in education spread rapidly through the states and even became a national political issue. In general, the prohibition against use of public funds for sectarian purposes became almost universal among the states by 1900, and the prohibition of religious instruction in the public schools was also widespread, especially among those new states that took express constitutional action. Among these were Wisconsin, Minnesota, Nevada, Colorado, Montana, Idaho, South Dakota, California, Arizona, Nebraska, and Wyoming.[36]

A close study of state constitutions, state statutes, and court decisions shows that the *principle* of separation of church and state in education was almost completely accepted throughout the United States by 1900. The one point that remained most in doubt as to *practice* was whether the reading of the Bible in public schools violated the principle of separation. Some courts ruled that the Bible was not sectarian instruction provided it was read without comment and if students who objected were excused from taking part. The decisions reflected the continuing belief among many persons that multiple establishment, if non-sectarian, was perfectly proper and would not violate freedom of worship and conscience. Other courts, however, have held exactly the opposite, that Bible reading *was* sectarian in the eyes of Catholics, Jews, and non-believers and therefore should be prohibited as unconstitutional because it in effect created a multiple establishment of religion.

One of the earliest and most important of these latter decisions came in the state of Ohio with respect to religious instruction in the public schools of Cincinnati. The board of education in Cincinnati had passed a resolution as follows:

Resolved, That religious instruction and the reading of religious books, including the Holy Bible, are prohibited in the common schools of Cincinnati, it being the true object and intent of this rule to allow the children of the parents of all sects and opinions, in matters of faith and worship, to enjoy alike the benefit of the common-school fund.[37]

A group of taxpayers brought action in the Superior Court of Cincinnati to enjoin the board of education from carrying out its resolution. The Superior Court ruled 2 to 1 against the board of education, but the board of education then appealed to the Ohio Supreme Court to reverse the decision. The Supreme Court reversed the lower courts and unanimously upheld the board of education in a notable decision, ruling that religious instruction was unconstitutional in the public schools of Ohio. The defendants had pointed out that the Constitution of Ohio, based upon an adaptation of the Northwest Ordinance of 1787, contained the following provision:

Religion, morality, and knowledge, however, being essential to good government, it shall be the duty of the general assembly to pass suitable laws to protect every religious denomination in the peaceable enjoyment of its own mode of public worship, and to encourage schools and the means of instruction.[38]

They argued from this that the public schools not only were permitted but were required to provide religious instruction in order to fulfill the injunction of the Constitution, irrespective of the wishes or consciences of the people concerned.

The court ruled, however, that the constitutional clause means that the word "knowledge" embraces all that is comprehended in "religion" and "morality" which can be the subject of *human* instruction. Therefore, nothing was enjoined upon the schools but to encourage the means of instruction in general "knowledge." Judge Welch argued that "religion" and "morality" are aided by the increase and diffusion of "knowledge" and that in this sense all three are essential to good government, but there is no direction given as to *what system of knowledge* should be taught or what is the *true* religion, morality, or knowledge. These matters are left to the legislature, subject to the limitations on legislative power regarding religious freedom as contained in the bill of rights. This limitation would prevent the legislature from defining or promoting religious doctrine. The court then points out that what the defendants are really arguing for is that "religion" means the *Christian* religion. This interpretation cannot be admitted for it would then establish Christianity as the law of the state:

Legal Christianity is a solecism, a contradiction of terms. When Christianity asks the aid of government beyond mere *impartial protection,* it denies itself. Its laws are divine, not human. Its essential interests lie beyond the reach and range of human governments. United with government, religion never rises above the merest superstition; united with religion, government never rises above the merest despotism; and all history shows us that the more widely and completely they are separated, the better it is for both.

Religion is not — much less is Christianity or any other particular system of religion — named in the preamble to the constitution of the United States as one of the declared *objects* of government; nor is it mentioned in the clause in question, in our own constitution, as being essential to anything *beyond* mere human government. . . .

Properly speaking, there is no such thing as "religion of state." What we mean by that phrase is, the religion of some individual or set of individuals, taught and enforced by the state. . . . If it embarks in this business, whose opinion shall it adopt . . . ?

If it be true that our law enjoins the teaching of the Christian religion in the schools, surely, then, all its teachers should be Christian . . . .

. . . But the real question here is, not what is the best religion, but how shall this best religion be secured? I answer, it can best be secured by adopting the doctrine of this 7th section in our own Bill of Rights, and which I summarize in two words, by calling it the doctrine of "hands off." Let the state not only keep its own hands off, but let it also see to it that religious sects keep their hands off each other.[39]

The court concludes by referring to Madison:

The principles here expressed are not new. . . . They are as old as Madison, and were his favorite opinions. Madison, who had more to do with framing the constitution of the United States than any other man, and whose purity of life and orthodoxy of religious belief no one questions, himself says:
"Religion is not within the purview of human government."[40]

This decision and many others that could be quoted place themselves in direct line with the principle of separation of church and state as developed over the past hundred years. When the court emphasized the neutrality of a government based upon *human* experience, it defined a *secular* basis for public education, a basis specifically not anti-religious nor irreligious, but a basis upon which the several religions then may build their own activities free from government interference. The court's reference to teachers is also significant.

What of the rights of conscience of a Catholic or Jewish teacher who is required to read the Protestant Bible to children of all faiths?

The achievement of complete separation in principle with regard to the use of public funds for sectarian schools was even more universally widespread by 1900. Building upon the start that had already been made prior to the Civil War the movement gained great headway following the Civil War. One of the reasons for this acceleration was the fact that the Roman Catholic Church redoubled its efforts to achieve a share of the public funds for its own parochial schools. This effort undoubtedly redoubled the efforts of other groups to prevent such outcome. These struggles took place on the national level as well as among the states. Action was so widespread and in general so uniform in intent, despite differences of wording in constitutions and statutes, that details cannot possibly be filled in here. Only two or three states could be said to be left with little protection.[41]

As the controversy began to heighten after the Civil War the State of Illinois led off with a provision in its new constitution of 1870 that sharply closed the door on the use of public funds "for any church or sectarian purpose" as follows:

Neither the general assembly nor any county, city, town, township, school district or other public corporation shall ever make any appropriation or pay from any public fund whatever, anything in aid of any church or sectarian purpose, or to help support or sustain any school, academy, seminary, college, university or other literary or scientific institution, controlled by any church or sectarian denomination whatever; nor shall any grant or donation of land, money or other personal property ever be made by the State or any such public corporation to any church or for any sectarian purpose.[42]

Some of the states did not act so comprehensively as did Illinois, but virtually all states included some constitutional provision to prohibit tax funds for sectarian purposes.

The final point to be made with respect to the latter part of the nineteenth century is to note the repercussions of this movement on the national political scene. Again, details cannot be described here, but certain developments may be pointed out. As the campaign for public funds for parochial schools took national proportions, it also took political form, for often the local and state Democratic parties became allied with the Catholic point of view or at least were not hostile. This meant that the Republican Party was not slow in taking the opposite stand. President Grant brought the issue into the national political arena in his speech to the Army of the Tennessee in Des Moines, Iowa in September 1875:

> Let us all labor to add all needful guarantees for the security of free thought, free speech, a free press, pure morals, unfettered religious sentiments, and of equal rights and privileges to all men, irrespective of nationality, color, or religion. Encourage free schools, and resolve that not one dollar appropriated for their support shall be appropriated to the support of any sectarian schools. Resolve that neither the State nor the nation, nor both combined, shall support institutions of learning other than those sufficient to afford every child growing up in the land the opportunity of a good common-school education, unmixed with sectarian, pagan, or atheistical dogmas. Leave the matter of religion to the family altar, the church, and the private school, supported entirely by private contributions. Keep the church and the state for ever separated.[43]

Following up this speech, Grant recommended specifically in his annual message to Congress of December 7, 1875 that an amendment to the Constitution be passed that would specifically prohibit any public funds for the direct or indirect aid of any religious sect and prohibit the teaching in public schools of any "religious, atheistic, or pagan tenets."[44]

James G. Blaine, as leader of the House, thereupon introduced a resolution to amend the Constitution by adding to the clauses of the First Amendment a specific and detailed statement that no funds of the United States, any state, territory, district, or municipality shall be used for the support of any school or other institution

under the control of any religious or anti-religious sect, organization, or denomination, or wherein the particular creed or tenets of any religious or anti-religious sect, organization, or denomination shall be taught. . . . This article shall not be construed to prohibit the reading of the Bible in any school or institution; and it shall not have the effect to impair rights of property already vested.[45]

On August 4, 1876 this resolution was passed by a large majority of the House. The section permitting Bible reading revealed the Protestant inspiration of the resolution, and the large number of abstentions in the voting revealed the difficulties many members of the House had in deciding a religious issue that had become so entangled in politics. The reference to "anti-religious" sects must have raised many questions concerning how a sect would be defined as anti-religious. The section on vested property rights also reveals the older conception of "due process" as discussed on page 105. The national election of 1876 was in full swing at this time during which the Republican national convention had inserted in its platform the following plank:

The public school system of the several States is the bulwark of the American Republic; and with a view to its security and permanence, we recommend an amendment to the Constitution of the United States forbidding the application of any public funds or property for the benefit of any school or institution under sectarian control.[46]

The partisan, sectional, and sectarian character of Blaine's proposal was still more clearly revealed when the Senate voted on the resolution; 27 Republicans favored, 16 Democrats against, and 27 senators not voting. The measure was lost because a two-thirds vote was required. It could be argued that this proposal showed that Republican leaders believed that the First Amendment as it stood was not sufficient to prevent public funds going to parochial schools, but it could just as well be argued that many legislators felt that such an amendment was unnecessary because the states were already adequately protecting public funds.[47]

Despite the failure in the Senate to gain concurrence for the Blaine resolution, the Congress nevertheless required that all new states, admitted to the Union after 1876, must adopt an irrevocable ordinance that not only guaranteed religious freedom but also required the states to include provision

for the establishment and maintenance of a system of public schools, which shall be open to all the children of said State and free from sectarian control; . . . .[48]

The Congress was thus reflecting the trend that by this time had begun to sweep the country to establish common school systems based upon separation of church and state and it lent the authority of the federal government to that movement.

One other aspect of the national struggle over the religious issue deserves to be mentioned. That has to do with the efforts to achieve federal aid for education in the Congress during the 1870's and 1880's. Much of the impetus behind the proposals of the Hoar bill of 1870 and the Blair bills of the 1880's came from Republican desires to stimulate the establishment of systems of common schools in the Southern states, but the religious issue was inevitably injected.[49] The Catholic Church opposed federal aid to the states if it were to be confined to public schools, but on occasion favored federal aid if it were to be divided "fairly" among public and parochial schools. Sufficient support to pass a federal aid bill was never achieved in both houses of Congress at once, so federal aid for general purposes of education had to wait until the twentieth century. Senator Blair blamed the Catholics for the defeat of federal aid and his parting shot was in the form of a proposed amendment in 1888 that would have required the states to maintain systems of public schools that included education "in the common branches of knowledge, and in virtue, morality, and the principles of the Christian religion."[50]

Fortunately for the principle of separation, this proposal for multiple establishment died in the fifty-first Congress, and within ten years Congress had enunciated a policy much more in line with the historical meaning of separation. In its appropriation acts for the District of Columbia in 1896 and 1897, Congress expressed a national policy in conformity with the policy of the vast majority of the states:

And it is hereby declared to be the policy of the Government of the United States to make no appropriation of money or property for the purpose of founding, maintaining, or aiding by payment for services, expenses, or otherwise, any church or religious denomination, or any institution or society which is under sectarian or ecclesiastical control; . . . .[51]

The Smith-Hughes Act of 1917 followed a similar pattern when it provided that

No portion of any moneys appropriated under this Act for the benefit of the States shall be applied, *directly or indirectly* . . . for the support of any religious or privately owned or conducted school or college.[52]

In the course of nearly 150 years of national and state history it had become clear to most Americans that the effort to achieve a common school in a religiously divided society required the separation of public funds from sectarian and religious institutions and instruction.

Since the beginning of the twentieth century the most noteworthy developments have been the increased efforts to reopen the question of separation and to gain greater "co-operation" between the church and state in education. The main outlines of the struggles that were precipitated by these efforts will be the subject of the next chapter.

6

The Struggle for Separation in Education in the Twentieth Century

IN THE FIRST HALF of the twentieth century the basic issues of conflict between church and state over education have remained the same but the location of the struggle has shifted. Most Americans continue to agree to the two general propositions that comprised the nineteenth century principle of separation of church and state in education. These were defined in Chapter 5 as follows:

(1) Public funds shall not be granted to sectarian schools.
(2) Sectarian religious instruction shall not be given in the public schools.

Most Americans continue to agree that these propositions constitute sound public policy in the realm of church and state relations but they do not agree concerning what the propositions mean for certain practices. This chapter will describe briefly the general lines of controversy that have raged about these two propositions in the twentieth century and will give examples of those practices that continue to raise knotty questions of educational and public policy.

SHALL PUBLIC FUNDS BE USED FOR SECTARIAN SCHOOLS?

The first proposition has taken a somewhat different form since 1900. Those who believe that more "co-operation" between church and state is desirable argue that, even though public funds may not be used *directly* to aid sectarian schools, public funds may be used and *should* be used to give aid to children who attend non-public schools. They argue that such aid is for the benefit of the individual child and is thus not an aid to the sectarian school as such. Such aid is a part of the "public welfare" benefits which the state should provide for all children no matter what school they attend. These benefits, now being described as "auxiliary services" or "fringe benefits," are justified on the ground that they do not aid the religious school and therefore they are within the permitted constitutional prerogatives of the federal or state governments. It is argued that they do not violate the principle of separation of church and state if *all* children are given the benefits without regard to the kind of private or religious school they attend.

In recent years this argument has taken still another form. Proponents of greater "co-operation" argue that so long as children are permitted to attend religious schools in fulfillment of the compulsory state attendance laws, the children have a right to all the benefits and services that are given to public school children. Otherwise, the children who attend non-public schools will be discriminated against because they exercise their rights of religious freedom guaranteed to them by the federal and state constitutions. The discrimination argument gains force when linked with growing concern for the achievement of full civil rights for all persons regardless of race, color, creed, or national origin.

With respect to the issue of public funds for sectarian schools it can thus be seen that the effort is no longer to gain public funds directly. That issue has been effectively settled at least for the present. No court of record shows cases involving direct aid to sectarian schools since 1900. The efforts in the past fifty years and especially in the past twenty years have been devoted to the effort to gain *indirect* support. By and large Roman Catholic groups have been the principal proponents of this drive for public funds for their parochial school system. When efforts to achieve direct aid proved unsuccessful, demands have been made for public funds to support educational activities not directly involving classroom teaching, such as public funds for transportation of children to parochial schools, free textbooks at public expense for children in parochial schools, free lunches for children in parochial schools, health and medical services for children in parochial schools, and the use of parochial school buildings and staff as public schools.[1] Financial support has been granted by several of the states on some of these issues. Such states would also be able to use federal funds for similar purposes under proposals to grant federal funds for any purpose for which the several states grant state funds. This provision was contained in the federal aid bill passed by the Senate in the eightieth Congress in 1948 and again in the eighty-first Congress in 1949.

Those who hold the opposing position argue that such "cooperation" as described above is really an entanglement or alliance that violates the historic principle of separation of church and state. They hold that sound public policy dictates less entanglement, not more. They insist that public aid to children who attend private and religious schools is *indirect* aid to the schools themselves and thus should be avoided, just as direct aid to the proprietors or faculty of the schools is avoided. Whatever public aid is given to the child helps him to receive religious instruction in religious schools, and this is using the public tax funds to help the religious schools promote their religious activities. Helping *all* religious groups in this way is as unconstitutional (multiple establishment) as is helping one religious group in preference to others (single establishment).

They argue that modern educational theory and practice view "auxiliary services" as integral parts of the total educational process and thus such services cannot be divorced from the instructional or curricular program of the schools. Transportation of children to a school where it is needed is as much a part of the instructional program as the payment of teachers' salaries. Free textbooks, even non-religious textbooks, when used in a religious setting in the hands of religiously trained teaching orders, are integral parts of a religious instructional program.

They hold that no charge of discrimination can legitimately be levelled at proposals to limit public funds to public school children. The public schools are open to all without regard to religious distinction. Any distinction on religious grounds that is made within the public schools would surely be unwise, unjust, and unconstitutional. But when any group voluntarily prefers to establish its own religious schools and when parents voluntarily choose to send their children to such schools, they cannot legitimately charge discrimination when public funds are withheld from those schools. It might as well be argued that because a person prefers to use a private club instead of a public park, or a private beach rather than a public beach, or a private doctor rather than a public clinic, he is therefore entitled to public support because he does not avail himself of the public facilities. Religious freedom to set up agencies of religious instruction does not require the use of public funds to support the exercise of that religious freedom. If a person prefers to set himself apart from public facilities that are freely available to him, he cannot charge discrimination when the public refuses to aid him in thus setting himself apart. If the American people persist in helping with public funds to build an ever stronger private school system they not only violate the principle of separation, they also help to weaken the public school system itself.

Thus the argument goes back and forth with respect to the use of public funds for children who attend private and religious schools. What the American people must now decide is whether or not the meaning of the historic principle of separation of church and state points to the prohibition of indirect aid to religious schools as clearly as it prohibits direct aid. Is indirect aid, equally to all religious schools, tantamount to multiple establishment of religion through "co-operation" of church and state? If the American people wish to adhere to separation of church and state, then the historical evidence presented in this book indicates that they should decide to prohibit indirect aid to children whose parents prefer to send them to sectarian or non-sectarian religious schools.

The question cannot be answered fully by simply referring to the past, because the issue of auxiliary services is a new problem brought about by changed conditions in society and in education. Bus transportation, free textbooks, health services, and school lunches were not on the educational scene when the issues of separation of church and state were decided in the nineteenth century. The historic principle of separation was decided before these new and fine distinctions arose, but the principle itself is clear from the study of history.

Aid to all religious groups is as clear a violation of separation as is aid to one religious group in preference to others. The line between direct aid and indirect aid is so difficult to draw that the American people would be well advised to stop short of indirect aid if they wish to avoid the entanglements that plagued the nation for well over a hundred years. Indirect aid is clearly moving toward greater "co-operation" between church and state, and greater "co-operation" between church and state has always brought the dangers of "an establishment of religion." Certain practices in education will be described to illustrate how these issues are involved.

Free Transportation

The problem of providing free transportation of children to religious schools obviously could not arise until the development of the automobile and the improvement of roads took place in the twentieth century. Then when the idea of consolidated school districts took hold, the small district school began to be replaced by central or consolidated schools to which pupils were transported by bus. At this point, especially following the First World War, the problem became acute and the drive to gain public funds for transportation of children to religious schools as well as to public schools gained momentum. As might be expected in a new and untried application of the principle of separation to educational matters, the practices varied from state to state or locality to locality. Laws varied and court decisions differed, reversals sometimes occurring within the same jurisdiction.

The actual status of providing bus transportation was a hodge-podge of varying practice with many fine distinctions being made among those states where the practice was permitted. By 1947 fourteen states had passed some sort of legislation enabling parochial school children to have access to transportation facilities along with public school children.[2] These states were California, Illinois, Indiana, Kentucky, Louisiana, Maryland, Massachusetts, Missouri, Michigan, New Hampshire, New Jersey, New York, Oregon, and Rhode Island. Transportation was permitted in four states by attorney general ruling (Colorado, Ohio, Vermont, and Wyoming), and in four states by ruling of the state department of education (Connecticut, Kansas, Montana, and New Mexico).

Thus, in twenty-two states some positive action has been taken on this issue, but variations in the extent of such aid are very wide. In only thirteen states may identifiable public funds be used in some form; in some states only local funds may be used; in others only public funds other than *school* funds; and in others no distinction is made. These thirteen states are Connecticut (if the town does not maintain a high school), Illinois, Kentucky, Louisiana, Maryland, Massachusetts, Missouri, New Hampshire (up to and including the ninth grade),

New Jersey, New York, Rhode Island, Vermont (permissible but not done), and Wyoming.

Five states permit parochial school pupils to use the public school buses if no extra cost is involved (Colorado, Kansas, Ohio, Michigan, New Mexico). Montana permits transportation of parochial school pupils if their parents pay a proportionate share of the cost. Transportation is permitted by two states if the private school is located along or near the regular school bus route (California and Oregon), and Indiana makes transportation mandatory on regular public school routes if no extra cost is involved. In these nine states the exact amount of expense to the public is difficult or impossible to determine. Obviously some compromises have been worked out in these states to accede to the demand of parochial school patrons for help in getting their children to religious schools, but these states have been unwilling to put them on an equal basis with public school children if an added expense is to be laid upon taxpayers. Questions must constantly arise concerning at what stage extra cost would be involved.

Most states have so far avoided these complicated questions by determining to provide transportation at public expense to public school children only. Most of the major court cases on the state level up to 1950 ruled that the use of public funds for transportation to parochial schools was unconstitutional; cases were so decided in eight states: Wisconsin (1923), South Dakota (1931), Delaware (1934), New York (1938), Oklahoma (1942), Kentucky (1942), Washington (1943 and 1949), and Iowa (1947). Court cases in four states went the other way: Maryland (1938 and 1942), New Jersey (1945), Kentucky (1945), and California (1946).

Two of these states changed their stand from disapproval to approval. New York amended its constitution to circumvent the New York decision of 1938, and the Kentucky court reversed itself in 1945. After the United States Supreme Court upheld the New Jersey decision in the Everson case, the state of New Jersey incorporated bus transportation for all children in its revised constitution of 1947. Thus, for a time it looked as though the earlier trend of court decisions against free transportation for parochial school children had begun to change, but the balance was maintained when Wisconsin refused to amend its constitution in a bitter referendum vote of 1946, and supreme court decisions in Iowa and Washington maintained their disapproval of free transportation despite the United States Supreme Court decision in the Everson case in 1947.

The basic issue in these court cases has been whether bus transportation at public expense for parochial school children is indirect aid to a religious school and therefore unconstitutional or whether it is merely general welfare legislation for the benefit of the individual child and thus not aid to the school. Excerpts from these cases on both sides are quoted here so that the line of reasoning of the different courts may be followed closely.

The state supreme courts that prohibited transportation for private school children argued as follows: The Wisconsin court held that

The whole scope and purpose of the statute is to comply with the provisions of the constitutional mandate, and that requires that free, nonsectarian instruction be provided for all persons of school age. The board is not authorized to expend public funds for any other purpose. *The contract made by the district board whereby it attempted to provide transportation of pupils to a private school was an act beyond its authority and therefore invalid.* . . . The school board is by statute authorized to provide transportation for such children of school age as desire to attend a public school and no others.[3]

In Delaware the court said:

We are of the opinion that *to furnish free transportation to pupils attending sectarian schools, is to aid the schools.* It helps build up, strengthen and make successful the schools as organizations.[4]

An important decision in New York went as follows:

While a close compact had existed between the Church and State in other governments, the Federal government and each State government from their respective beginnings have followed the new concept whereby the State deprived itself of all control over religion and has refused sectaries any participation in or jurisdiction or control over the civil prerogatives of the State. And so *in all civil affairs there has been a complete separation of Church and State jealously guarded and unflinchingly maintained.* In conformity with that concept, education in State supported schools must be non-partisan and non-sectarian. *This involves no discrimination between individuals or classes. It invades the religious rights of no one.* While education is compulsory in this State between certain ages, the State has no desire to and could not if it so wished compel children to attend the free public schools when their parents desire to send them to parochial schools (Pierce v. Society of the Sisters of the Holy Names of Jesus and Mary, 268 U.S. 510) . . . but their *attendance upon the parochial school or private school is a matter of choice and the cost thereof not a matter of public concern.*[5] . . .

Aid or support to the school "directly or indirectly" is proscribed. The two words must have been used with some definite intent and purpose; otherwise why were they used at all? Aid furnished "directly" would be that furnished in a direct line, both literally and figuratively, to the school itself, unmistakably earmarked, and without circumlocution or ambiguity. *Aid furnished "indirectly" clearly embraces any contribution, to whomsoever made, circuitously, collaterally, disguised, or otherwise not in a straight, open and direct course for the open and avowed aid of the school, that may be to the benefit of the institution or promotional of its interests and purposes.* How could the people have expressed their purpose in the fundamental law in more apt, simple and all-embracing language? Free transportation of pupils induced attendance at the school. *The purpose of the transportation is to promote the interests of the private school or religious or sectarian institution that controls and directs it.* . . . Without pupils there could be no school. It is illogical to say that the furnishing of transportation is not an aid to the institution while the employment of teachers and furnishing of books, accommodations and other facilities are such an aid. In the instant case, $3,350 was appropriated out of public moneys solely for the transportation of the relatively few pupils attending the specific school in question. *If the cardinal rule that written constitutions are to receive uniform and unvarying interpretation and practical construction is to be followed, in view of interpretation in analogous cases it cannot successfully be maintained that the furnishing of transportation to the private or parochial school out of public money is not in aid or support of the school.*[6]

The Oklahoma court held that

The appropriation and directed use of public funds in transportation of public school children is openly in direct aid to public schools "as such." When such aid is purported to be extended to a sectarian school there is in our judgment a clear violation of the above-quoted provisions (Section 5, Article 2) of our Constitution.[7]

The Supreme Court of Kentucky ruled that

The portion of school law requiring that pupils attending private school be given the same transportation rights as pupils of public schools violates constitutional provision requiring that taxes be levied and collected for "public purposes" only and that no sum should be collected for education other than in "common schools" until question of taxation is submitted to legal voters, as against claim that statute was for the aid of children, and not private schools.[8]

It is obvious that the Louisiana case and a few others of similar import relied on for defendants are contrary to the great weight of authority, and are lacking in persuasive reasoning and logic. We are of the opinion, therefore, that the Act here under consideration is unconstitutional and therefore void.[9]

The state of Washington court said:

We cannot . . . accept the validity of the argument that transportation of pupils to and from school is not beneficial to, and in aid of, the school. *Even legislation providing for transportation of pupils to and from the public school is constitutionally defensible only as the exercise of a governmental function furthering the maintenance and development of the common school system. . . .*
We think the conclusion is inescapable that free transportation

of pupils serves to aid and build up the school itself. That pupils and parents may also derive benefit from it, is beside the question.[10]

The state supreme courts that upheld free transportation argued that it was a legitimate exercise of the police power of the state for the benefit of the child and in the service of a public function. Maryland was one of the earliest to apply this argument to transportation:

Starting with the interest which the state is acknowledged to have in seeing that all children of school age acquire an education by attending some school, and the fact that they are complying with the law in going to such a school as the parochial school involved in this case, their accommodation in the buses appears to the court to be within the proper limits of enforcement of the duty imposed.[11]

In 1945 Kentucky's court reversed its earlier stand by arguing that

. . . [The act] constitutes simply what it purports to be — *an exercise of police power for the protection of childhood against the inclemency of the weather and from the hazards of present-day highway traffic.*[12]
. . . *the fact that in a strained and technical sense the school might derive an indirect benefit from the enactment, is not sufficient to defeat the declared purpose and the practical and wholesome effect of the law.*[13]

California also followed the police power argument:

Raising the standard of intelligence of youth and providing for the safety of children are legitimate objects of government and are authorized under the police powers. It is also true that the transportation of pupils to and from public schools is one of the legitimate methods adopted to help promote education and safeguard children. If the transportation of pupils to and from public schools is authorized, as it certainly is, and *if the benefit from that transportation is to the pupils, then an incidental benefit flowing to a denominational school from free transportation of its pupils should not be sufficient to deprive the legislature of the power to authorize a school district to transport such pupils.*[14]

These state court decisions had been decided largely in terms of state constitutions, but the question took the form of a federal issue when the Everson case was appealed from the New Jersey courts to the United States Supreme Court on the grounds that the First Amendment had been violated. In the Supreme Court's close decision of February 10, 1947, the majority of five upheld the line of argument of the three state courts cited above that the state's police power in providing general welfare legislation for the benefit of the child superseded the prohibition against "an establishment of religion" of the First Amendment. The minority of four, however, held that the "general welfare" argument was beside the point and neglected the whole meaning of the First Amendment which was the only basis upon which the Supreme Court had jurisdiction. The minority followed the reasoning of the eight court decisions cited above. The two divergent stands represented by the state court decisions were thus represented in the Supreme Court's majority and minority opinions. Excerpts from both the majority and minority will be quoted here in order that they may be seen in the light of the historical evidence presented in the foregoing chapters of this book.

The majority opinion, written by Mr. Justice Black, defines its general interpretation of the meaning of the First Amendment as follows:

The "establishment of religion" clause of the First Amendment means at least this: Neither a state nor the Federal Government can set up a church. *Neither can pass laws which aid one religion, aid all religions, or prefer one religion over another.* Neither can force nor influence a person to go to or to remain away from church against his will or force him to profess a belief or disbelief in any religion. No person can be punished for entertaining or professing religious beliefs or disbeliefs, for church attendance or non-attendance. *No tax in any amount, large or small, can be levied to support any religious activities or institutions, whatever they may be called, or whatever form they may adopt to teach or practice religion.* Neither a state nor the Federal Government can, openly or secretly, participate in the affairs of any religious organizations or groups and *vice versa*. In the words of Jefferson, the clause against establishment of religion by law was intended to erect "a wall of separation between church and State."[15]

The foregoing statement is clearly in line with the historic meaning of separation which outlaws multiple as well as single establishments. The majority opinion goes on, however, to argue that public funds to the individual child come under the heading of public welfare legislation and thus are not prohibited by the First Amendment, although a state could if it so wishes refuse such aid. In its practical application of the principle, or rather in its failure to apply the principle, the majority opinion departed from the historic meaning of separation as defined in the earlier chapters of this book:

We must consider the New Jersey statute in accordance with the foregoing limitations imposed by the First Amendment. But we must not strike that state statute down if it is within the State's constitutional power even though it approaches the verge of that power. See *Interstate Ry. v. Massachusetts,* Holmes, J., *supra* at 85, 88. New Jersey cannot consistently with the "establishment of religion" clause of the First Amendment contribute tax-raised funds to the support of an institution which teaches the tenets and faith of any church. On the other hand, other language of the amendment commands that New Jersey cannot hamper its citizens in the free exercise of their own religion. Consequently, it cannot exclude individual Catholics, Lutherans, Mohammedans, Baptists, Jews, Methodists, Non-believers, Presbyterians, or the members of any other faith, *because of their faith, or lack of it,* [Italics the Court's] from receiving the benefits of public welfare legislation. *While we do not mean to intimate that a state could not provide transportation only to children attending public schools, we must be careful,* in protecting the citizens of New Jersey against state-established churches, *to be sure that we do not inadvertently prohibit New Jersey from extending its general state law benefits to all its citizens without regard to their religious belief.*

Measured by these standards, we cannot say that the First Amendment prohibits New Jersey from spending tax-raised funds to pay the bus fares of parochial school pupils as a part of a general program under which it pays the fares of pupils attending public and other schools. It is undoubtedly true that children are helped to get to church schools. There is even a possibility that some of the children might not be sent to the church schools if the parents were compelled to pay their children's bus fares out of their own pockets when transportation to a public school would have been paid for by the State. The same possibility exists where the state requires a local transit company to provide reduced fares to school children including those attending parochial schools, or where a municipally owned transportation system undertakes to carry all school children free of charge. Moreover, state-paid policemen, detailed to protect children going to and from church schools from the very real hazards of traffic, would serve much the same purpose and accomplish much the same result as state provisions intended to guarantee free transportation of a kind which the state deems to be best for the school children's welfare. And parents might refuse to risk their children to the serious danger of traffic accidents going to and from parochial schools, the approaches to which were not protected by policemen. Similarly, parents might be reluctant to permit their children to attend schools which the state had cut off from such general government services as ordinary police and fire protection, connections for sewage disposal, public highways and sidewalks. Of course, cutting off church schools from these services, so separate and so indisputably marked off from the religious function, would make it far more difficult for the schools to operate. But such is obviously not the purpose of the First Amendment. *That Amendment requires the state to be a neutral in its relations with groups of religious believers and non-believers; it does not require the state to be their adversary. State power is no more to be used so as to handicap religions than it is to favor them.*

This Court has said that parents may, in the discharge of their duty under state compulsory education laws, send their children to a religious rather than a public school if the school meets the secular educational requirements which the state has power to impose. See *Pierce v. Society of Sisters,* 268 U. S. 510. It appears that these parochial schools meet New Jersey's requirements. The State contributes no money to the schools. It does not support them. *Its legislation, as applied, does no more than provide a general program to help parents get their children, regardless of their religion, safely and expeditiously to and from accredited schools.*

The First Amendment has erected a wall between church and state. That wall must be kept high and impregnable. We could not approve the slightest breach. New Jersey has not breached it here.[16]

The minority opinion, written by Mr. Justice Rutledge, agreed that the First Amendment rules out multiple as well as single establishment, but argued that the logic of this meaning would require that no public funds be used for transportation of parochial school pupils on the grounds that such aid is an establishment of religion. Such aid promotes religion, and thus, even though it is designed as public welfare legislation, it does exactly what the First Amendment prohibits:

Neither so high nor so impregnable today as yesterday is the wall raised between church and state by Virginia's great statute of religious freedom and the First Amendment, now made applicable to all the states by the Fourteenth. New Jersey's statute sustained is the first, if indeed it is not the second breach to be made by this Court's action. That a third, and a fourth, and still others will be attempted, we may be sure. For just as *Cochran v. Board of Education,* 281 U. S. 370, has opened the way by oblique ruling for this decision, so will the two make wider the breach for a third. Thus with time the most solid freedom steadily gives way before continuing corrosive decision. . . .

The Amendment's purpose was not to strike merely at the official establishment of a single sect, creed or religion, outlawing only a formal relation such as had prevailed in England and some of the colonies. Necessarily it was to uproot all such relationships. *But the object was broader than separating church and state in this narrow sense. It was to create a complete and permanent separation of the spheres of religious activity and civil authority by comprehensively forbidding every form of public aid or support for religion. In proof the Amendment's wording and history unite with this Court's consistent utterances whenever attention has been fixed directly upon the question.*

"Religion" appears only once in the Amendment. But the word governs two prohibitions and governs them alike. It does not have two meanings, one narrow to forbid "an establishment" and another, much broader, for securing "the free exercise thereof."

"Thereof" brings down "religion" with its entire and exact content, no more and no less, from the first into the second guaranty, so that Congress and now the states are as broadly restricted concerning the one as they are regarding the other. . . .

. . . Accordingly, daily religious education commingled with secular is "religion" within the guaranty's comprehensive scope. So are religious training and teaching in whatever form. The word connotes the broadest content, determined not by the form or formality of the teaching or where it occurs, but by its essential nature regardless of those details.

"Religion" has the same broad significance in the twin prohibition concerning "an establishment." The Amendment was not duplicitous. "Religion" and "establishment" were not used in any formal or technical sense. *The prohibition broadly forbids state support, financial or other, of religion in any guise, form or degree. It outlaws all use of public funds for religious purposes.*[17]

With this broad definition of "an establishment of religion," which agrees with the majority opinion and with the historical facts, the minority opinion went on to apply this meaning to the use of public funds for transportation of children to a religious school:

Does New Jersey's action furnish support for religion by use of the taxing power? Certainly it does, if the test remains undiluted as Jefferson and Madison made it, that money taken by taxation from one is not to be used or given to support another's religious training or belief, or indeed one's own. Today as then the furnishing of "contributions of money for the propagation of opinions which he disbelieves" is the forbidden exaction; and the prohibition is absolute for whatever measure brings that consequence and whatever amount may be sought or given to that end.

The funds used here were raised by taxation. The Court does not dispute, nor could it, that their use does in fact give aid and encouragement to religious instruction. It only concludes that this aid is not "support" in law. But Madison and Jefferson were concerned with aid and support in fact, not as a legal conclusion "entangled in precedents." Remonstrance, Par. 3. *Here parents pay money to send their children to parochial schools and funds raised by taxation are used to reimburse them. This not only helps the children to get to school and the parents to send them. It aids them in a substantial way to get the very thing which they are sent to the particular school to secure, namely, religious training and teaching.*

Believers of all faiths, and others who do not express their feeling toward ultimate issues of existence in any creedal form, pay the New Jersey tax. When the money so raised is used to pay for transportation to religious schools, the Catholic taxpayer to the extent of his proportionate share pays for the transportation of Lutheran, Jewish and otherwise religiously affiliated children to receive their non-Catholic religious instruction. Their parents likewise pay proportionately for the transportation of Catholic children to receive Catholic instruction. Each thus contributes to "the propagation of opinions which he disbelieves" in so far as their religions differ, as do others who accept no creed without regard to those differences. Each thus pays taxes also to support the teaching of his own religion, an exaction equally forbidden since it denies "the comfortable liberty" of giving one's contribution to the particular agency of instruction he approves.

New Jersey's action therefore exactly fits the type of exaction and the kind of evil at which Madison and Jefferson struck. Under the test they framed it cannot be said that the cost of transportation is no part of the cost of education or of the religious instruction given. That it is a substantial and a necessary element is shown most plainly by the continuing and increasing demand for the state to assume it. Nor is there pretense that it relates only to the secular and the religious instruction. It is precisely because the instruction is religious and relates to a particular faith, whether one or another, that parents send their children to religious schools under the *Pierce* doctrine. *And the very purpose of the state's contribution is to defray the cost of conveying the pupil to the place where he will receive not simply secular, but also and primarily religious, teaching and guidance.*

Indeed the view is sincerely avowed by many of various faiths, that the basic purpose of all education is or should be religious, that the secular cannot be and should not be separated from the religious phase and emphasis. Hence, the inadequacy of public or secular education and the necessity for sending the child to a school where religion is taught. But whatever may be the philosophy or its justification, there is undeniably an admixture of religious with secular teaching in all such institutions. That is the very reason for their being. Certainly for purposes of constitutionality we cannot contradict the whole basis of the ethical and educational convictions of people who believe in religious schooling.

Yet this very admixture is what was disestablished when the First Amendment forbade "an establishment of religion." Commingling the religious with the secular teaching does not divest the whole of its religious permeation and emphasis or make them of minor part, if proportion were material. Indeed, on any other view, the constitutional prohibition always could be brought to naught by adding a modicum of the secular.

An appropriation from the public treasury to pay the cost of transportation to Sunday school, to weekday special classes at the church or parish house, or to the meetings of various young people's religious societies, such as the Y. M. C. A., the Y. W. C. A., the Y. M. H. A., the Epworth League, could not withstand the constitutional attack. This would be true, whether or not secular activities were mixed with the religious. If such an appropriation could not stand, then it is hard to see how one becomes valid for the same thing upon the more extended scale of daily instruction. Surely constitutionality does not turn on where or how often the mixed teaching occurs.

Finally, transportation, where it is needed, is as essential to education as any other element. Its cost is as much a part of the total expense, except at times in amount, as the cost of textbooks, of school lunches, of athletic equipment, of writing and other materials; indeed of all other items composing the total burden. Now as always the core of the educational process is the teacher-pupil relationship. Without this the richest equipment and facilities would go for naught. See *Judd v. Board of Education,* 278 N. Y. 200, 212. . . . But the proverbial Mark Hopkins conception no longer suffices for the country's requirements. *Without buildings, without equipment, without library, textbooks and other materials, and without transportation to bring teacher and pupil together in such an effective teaching environment, there can be not even the skeleton of what our times require.* Hardly can it be maintained that transportation is the least essential of these items, or that it does not in fact aid, encourage, sustain and support, just as they do, the very process which is its purpose to accomplish. No less essential is it, or the payment of its cost, than the very teaching in the classroom or payment of the teacher's sustenance. Many types of equipment, now considered essential, better could be done without.

For me, therefore, the feat is impossible to select so indispensable an item from the composite of total costs, and characterize it as not aiding, contributing to, promoting or sustaining the propagation of beliefs which it is the very end of all to bring about. Unless this can be maintained, and the Court does not maintain it, the aid thus given is outlawed. *Payment of transportation is no more, nor is it any the less essential to education, whether religious or secular, than payment for tuitions, for teachers' salaries, for buildings, equipment and necessary materials.* Nor is it any the less directly related, in a school giving religious instruction, to the primary religious objective all those essential items of cost are intended to achieve. No rational line can be drawn between payment for such larger, but not more necessary, items and payment for transportation. The only line that can be so drawn is one between more dollars and less. Certainly in this realm such a line can be no valid constitutional measure. *Murdock v. Pennsylvania,* 319 U. S. 105; *Thomas v. Collins,* 323 U. S. 516. Now, as in Madison's time, not the amount but the principle of assessment is wrong. Remonstrance, Par. 3.

But we are told that the New Jersey statute is valid in its present application because the appropriation is for a public, not a private purpose, namely, the promotion of education, and the majority accept this idea in the conclusion that all we have here is "public welfare legislation." If that is true and the Amendment's force can be thus destroyed, what has been said becomes all the more pertinent. For then there could be no possible objection to more extensive support of religious education by New Jersey.

If the fact alone be determinative that religious schools are engaged in education, thus promoting the general and individual welfare, together with the legislature's decision that the payment of public moneys for their aid makes their work a public function, then *I can see no possible basis,* except one of dubious legislative policy, *for the state's refusal to make full appropriation for support of private, religious schools, just as is done for public instruction.* There could not be, on that basis, valid constitutional objection.

Of course paying the cost of transportation promotes the general cause of education and the welfare of the individual. So does paying all other items of educational expense. And obviously, as the majority say, it is much too late to urge that legislation designed to facilitate the opportunities of children to secure education serves no public purpose. Our nation-wide system of public education rests on the contrary view, as do all grants in aid of education, public or private, which is not religious in character.

These things are beside the real question. They have no possible materiality except to obscure the all-pervading, inescapable issue. Cf. Cochran v. Board of Education, supra. Stripped of its religious phase, the case presents no substantial federal question. Ibid. The public function argument, by casting the issue in terms of promoting the general cause of education and the welfare of the individual, ignores the religious factor and its essential connection with the transportation, thereby leaving out the only vital element in the case. So of course do the "public welfare" and "social legislation" ideas, for they come to the same thing.

This is not therefore just a little case over bus fares. In paraphrase of Madison, distant as it may be in its present form from a complete establishment of religion, it differs from it only in degree; and is the first step in that direction.[18]

Mr. Justice Rutledge insisted that discrimination does not result from denying transportation aid to parochial school children:

No one conscious of religious values can be unsympathetic toward the burden which our constitutional separation puts on parents who desire religious instruction mixed with secular for their children. They pay taxes for others' children's education, at the same time the added cost of instruction for their own. Nor can one happily see benefits denied to children which others receive, because in conscience they or their parents for them desire a different kind of training others do not demand.

But if those feelings should prevail, there would be an end to our historic constitutional policy and command. No more unjust or discriminatory in fact is it to deny attendants at religious schools the cost of their transportation than it is to deny them tuition, sustenance for their teachers, or any other educational expense which others receive at public cost. Hardship in fact there is which none can blink. But, for assuring to those who undergo it the greater, the most comprehensive freedom, it is one written by design and firm intent into our basic law.

Of course discrimination in the legal sense does not exist. The child attending the religious school has the same right as any other to attend the public school. But he foregoes exercising it because the same guaranty which assures this freedom forbids the public school or any agency of the state to give or aid him in securing the religious instruction he seeks.

Were he to accept the common school, he would be the first to protest the teaching there of any creed or faith not his own. And it is precisely for the reason that their atmosphere is wholly secular that children are not sent to public schools under the *Pierce* doctrine. But that is a constitutional necessity, because *we have staked the very existence of our country on the faith that complete separation between the state and religion is best for the state and best for religion.* Remonstrance, Par. 8, 12.

That policy necessarily entails hardship upon persons who forego the right to educational advantages the state can supply in order to secure others it is precluded from giving. Indeed this may hamper the parent and the child forced by conscience to that choice. *But it does not make the state unneutral to withhold what the Constitution forbids it to give. On the contrary it is only by observing the prohibition rigidly that the state can maintain its neutrality and avoid partisanship in the dissensions inevitable when sect opposes sect over demands for public moneys to further religious education, teaching or training in any form or degree, directly or indirectly.* Like St. Paul's freedom, religious liberty with a great price must be bought. And for those who exercise it most fully, by insisting upon religious education for their children mixed with secular, by the terms of our Constitution the price is greater than for others.[19]

Finally, Rutledge correctly saw that multiple establishment is outlawed by the principle of separation along with single establishment:

The problem then cannot be cast in terms of legal discrimination or its absence. This would be true, even though the state in giving aid should treat all religious instruction alike. Thus, if the present statute and its application were shown to apply equally to all religious schools of whatever faith, yet in the light of our tradition it could not stand. For then the adherent of one creed still would pay for the support of another, the childless taxpayer with others more fortunate. Then too there would seem to be no bar to making appropriations for transportation and other expenses of children attending public or other secular schools, after hours in separate places and classes for their exclusively religious instruction. The person who embraces no creed also would be forced to pay for teaching what he does not believe. Again, it was the furnishing of "contributions of money for the propagation of opinions which he disbelieves" that the fathers outlawed. *That consequence and effect are not removed by multiplying to all-inclusiveness the sects for which support is exacted. The Constitution requires, not comprehensive identification of state with religion, but complete separation.* [20]

In a separate dissenting opinion Mr. Justice Jackson effectively stated a position that corresponded with that of Rutledge:

It is of no importance in this situation whether the beneficiary of this expenditure of tax-raised funds is primarily the parochial school and incidentally the pupil, or whether the aid is directly bestowed on the pupil with indirect benefits to the school. The state cannot maintain a Church and it can no more tax its citizens to furnish free carriage to those who attend a Church. *The prohibition against establishment of religion cannot be circumvented by a subsidy, bonus or reimbursement of expense to individuals for receiving religious instruction and indoctrination. . . .*

Of course, the state may pay out tax-raised funds to relieve pauperism, but it may not under our Constitution do so to induce or reward piety. It may spend funds to secure old age against want, but it may not spend funds to secure religion against skepticism. It may compensate individuals for loss of employment, but it cannot compensate them for adherence to a creed.

It seems to me that the basic fallacy in the Court's reasoning, which accounts for its failure to apply the principles it avows, is in ignoring the essentially religious test by which beneficiaries of this expenditure are selected. A policeman protects a Catholic, of course — but not because he is a Catholic; it is because he is a man and a member of our society. The fireman protects the Church school — but not because it is a Church school; it is because it is property, part of the assets of our society. Neither the fireman nor the policeman has to ask before he renders aid "Is this man or building identified with the Catholic Church?" . . . I agree that this Court has left, and always should leave to each state, great latitude in deciding for itself, in the light of its own conditions, what shall be public purposes in its scheme of things. It may socialize utilities and economic enterprises and make taxpayers' business out of what conventionally had been private business. *It may make public business of individual welfare, health, education, entertainment or security. But it cannot make public business of religious worship or instruction, or of attendance at religious institutions of any character.* There is no answer to the proposition, more fully expounded by MR. JUSTICE RUTLEDGE, that the effect of the religious freedom Amendment to our Constitution was to take every form of propagation of religion out of the realm of things which could directly or indirectly be made public business and thereby be supported in whole or in part at taxpayers' expense. *That is a difference which the Constitution sets up between religion and almost every other subject matter of legislation, a difference which goes to the very root of religious freedom and which the Court is overlooking today. . . .*

This policy of our Federal Constitution has never been wholly pleasing to most religious groups. They all are quick to invoke its protections; they all are irked when they feel its restraints. . . .

But we cannot have it both ways. Religious teaching cannot be a private affair when the state seeks to impose regulations which infringe on it indirectly, and a public affair when it comes to taxing citizens of one faith to aid another, or those of no faith to aid all. If these principles seem harsh in prohibiting aid to Catholic education, it must not be forgotten that it is the same Constitution that alone assures Catholics the right to maintain these schools at all when predominant local sentiment would forbid them. *Pierce v. Society of Sisters,* 268 U. S. 510. Nor should I think that those who have done so well without this aid would want to see this separation between Church and State broken down. *If the state may aid these religious schools, it may therefore regulate them.* Many groups have sought aid from tax funds only to find that it carried political controls with it. Indeed this Court has declared that "It is hardly lack of due process for the Government to regulate that which it subsidizes." *Wickard v. Filburn,* 317 U. S. 111, 131.

But in any event, the great purposes of the Constitution do not depend on the approval or convenience of those they restrain. I cannot read the history of the struggle to separate political from ecclesiastical affairs, well summarized in the opinion of MR. JUSTICE RUTLEDGE in which I generally concur, without a conviction that the Court today is unconsciously giving the clock's hands a backward turn.[21]

When the arguments of the majority and minority opinions are thus seen in historical perspective, it seems clear that the minority opinion rests more securely upon a sound historical interpretation of the meaning of establishment. Indirect aid for the support of religion is an establishment of religion as fully as is direct aid. The majority decision in the Everson case may now open the way for increased efforts in the states to obtain transportation for parochial school children. Moreover, the prospect of federal aid to education will stimulate the drive to divert larger and larger amounts of public funds into indirect aid of sectarian education. Those who are concerned with the future of religious freedom and of public education may properly ask where will it end and what will become of the meaning of separation of church and state? The historical evidence points to the minority opinion as a sound basis for wise public policy as choices confront the people of the several states.

The two most recent state supreme court decisions took this position when they followed the minority opinion of the Everson case rather than the majority. The Iowa supreme court upheld the lower courts and the attorney general's ruling that transportation to parochial schools was unconstitutional:

We believe that the school laws of the state concern only the public schools unless otherwise expressly indicated, and do and can apply only to the schools within the purview of the school statutes, or under the control or jurisdiction of school officials, and that this would apply to transportation.[22]

The Washington Supreme Court in 1949 specifically rejected the Everson majority and asserted that the Washington Constitution ruled out transportation of children to religious schools at public expense:

Our own state constitution provides that no public money or property shall be used in support of institutions wherein the tenets of a particular religion are taught. Although the decisions of the United States supreme court are entitled to the highest consideration as they bear on related questions before this court, we must, in light of the clear provisions of our state constitution and our decisions thereunder, respectfully disagree with those portions of the Everson majority opinion which might be construed, in the abstract, as stating that transportation, furnished at public expense, to children attending religious schools, is not *in support* of such schools. While the degree of support necessary to constitute an establishment of religion under the First Amendment to the Federal constitution is foreclosed from consideration by reason of the decision in the Everson case, supra, we are constrained to hold that the Washington constitution although based upon the same precepts, is a clear denial of the rights herein asserted by appellants.[23]

Free Textbooks

Although the practice of providing textbooks at public expense for children in religious schools is much less widespread than transportation, it has been important because of the "child benefit" principle involved in some of the prominent court cases on this subject. In 1947 only five states used public funds to provide free textbooks to parochial school children. These were Louisiana, Mississippi, New Mexico, Oregon, and West Virginia. If federal aid should allow federal funds to be used for such auxiliary services as free textbooks the practice would undoubtedly spread among the states.

One of the earliest modern court cases to be decided on this issue was in New York in 1922 when the court held that furnishing books to pupils in parochial schools was a violation of the constitutional separation of church and state:

The school is not the building and its equipment; it is the organization, the union of all the elements in the organization, to furnish education in some branch of learning. . . . It is the institution, and the teachers and scholars together, that make it up. The pupils are a part of the school. . . . *It seems to us to be giving a strained and unusual meaning to words if we hold that the books and the ordinary school supplies, when furnished for the use of pupils, is a furnishing to the pupils, and not a furnishing in aid or maintenance of a school of learning. It seems very plain that such furnishing is at least indirectly in aid of the institution, and that, if not in actual violation of the words, it is in violation of the true intent and meaning, of the Constitution, and in consequence equally unconstitutional.*[24]

Two other important court cases, however, went the other way, one in Louisiana and one in Mississippi. The Cochran case in Louisiana was especially important for the formulation of the "child benefit" theory which was later upheld in the United States Supreme Court in 1930.

The Louisiana supreme court had argued that the textbooks went to the child and thus did not aid the school:

One may scan the acts in vain to ascertain where any money is appropriated for the purchase of school books for the use of any church, private, sectarian, or even public school. The appropriations were made for the specific purpose of purchasing school books for the use of the school children of the state, free of cost to them. *It was for their benefit and the resulting benefit to the state that the appropriations were made.* True, these children attend some school, public or private, the latter, sectarian or non-sectarian, and that the books are to be furnished them for their use, free of cost, whichever they attend. *The schools, however, are not the beneficiaries of these appropriations.* It is also true that the sectarian schools, which some of the children attend, instruct their pupils in religion, and books are used for that purpose, but one may search diligently the acts, though without result, in an effort to find anything to the effect that it is the purpose of the state to furnish religious books for the use of such children. . . . *What the statutes contemplate is that the same books that are furnished children attending public schools shall be furnished children attending private schools.* This is the only practical way of interpreting and executing the statutes, and this is what the state board of education is doing. Among these books, naturally, none is to be expected adapted to religious instruction.[25]

The opinion of the Supreme Court of the United States on the Cochran case, written by Chief Justice Hughes, upheld the Louisiana court under the due process clause of the Fourteenth Amendment, arguing that the textbooks served a public rather than a private function. The issue of the First Amendment was not raised:

Viewing the statute as having the effect thus attributed to it, *we can not doubt that the taxing power of the State is exerted for a public purpose.* The legislation does not segregate private schools, or their pupils, as its beneficiaries or attempt to interfere with any matters of exclusively private concern. Its interest is education, broadly; its method, comprehensive. Individual interests are aided only as the common interest is safeguarded.[26]

Thus it can be seen that the Cochran case affirmed a principle that did not involve the First Amendment. This fact makes it all the more clear that the majority opinion in the Everson case neglected the essentially religious aspect of the question of auxiliary services, as the minority in Everson claimed:

If it is part of the state's function to supply to religious schools or their patrons the smaller items of educational expense, because the legislature may say they perform a public function, it is hard to see why the larger ones also may not be paid. Indeed, it would seem even more proper and necessary for the state to do this. For if one class of expenditures is justified on the ground that it supports the general cause of education or benefits the individual, or can be made to do so by legislative declaration, so even more certainly would be the other. To sustain payment for transportation to school, for textbooks, for other essential materials, or perhaps for school lunches, and not for what makes all these things effective for their intended end, would be to make a public function of the smaller items and their cumulative effect, but to make wholly private in character the larger things without which the smaller could have no meaning or use.[27]

Federal Aid to Education

The question of providing public funds for such indirect aid or "auxiliary services" to parochial school children as transportation, textbooks, and health services became a national issue rather than simply state-wide when federal aid to education entered the picture. Here, above all, should the historical evidence be kept clearly in the forefront of public policy-making. The proponents of separation argue that unless the principle is upheld that indirect aid to parochial schools is an establishment of religion along with direct aid, there is no logical stopping point in providing non-instructional services. If public and parochial schools share alike, except for payment of teachers' salaries, what is to prevent payment of public funds to private schools for school buildings, operation and maintenance costs, libraries, recreation, equipment, and other expenses in addition to health and medical care, transportation, and textbooks? Indeed, if the child's needs for education are the only consideration and are to be divorced from the religious question, why not provide for teachers' salaries too? This is the logic of the "child benefit" theory as held by proponents of "co-operation" between church and state. This logic could easily be derived from the decision of a Mississippi court in 1941 which followed the lead of the Cochran case in Louisiana:

The religion to which children of school age adhere is not subject to control by the state; but the children themselves are subject to its control. *If the pupil may fulfil its duty to the state by attending a parochial school it is difficult to see why the state may not fulfil its duty to the pupil by encouraging it "by all suitable means."* The state is under a duty to ignore the child's creed, but not its need. It cannot control what one child may think, but it can and must do all it can to teach the child how to think. The state which allows the pupil to subscribe to any religious creed should not, because of his exercise of this right, proscribe him from benefits common to all.[28]

The details of the struggle over federal aid in recent years cannot be considered here in detail.[29] It is clearly evident, however, that the religious controversy has been one of the major stumbling blocks which has delayed the passage of federal aid bills since the First World War. Now it can no longer be denied that the religious issue has become the foremost cause of delay in federal aid since the end of the Second World War. The basic issue has been whether or not "auxiliary services" for non-public schools should be included in federal aid along with funds for public schools.

This issue in its extreme forms has been defined as follows: One position has said that federal aid should go to public schools only; the other position has said that federal aid should go equally or fairly to public and parochial schools alike. However, neither of these extreme views could make much headway. Then in the seventy-ninth Congress in 1946 the issue was defined somewhat differently, and a formula was worked out to allow the states to decide for what purposes federal aid should be used, on the basis that each state could use federal funds for any purpose for which state funds could constitutionally and legally be used. This formula was embodied in an amendment to the Senate bill S181 supported by the National Education Association. In opposition to this bill was S2499 which provided that federal funds could be used for such non-instructional purposes as transportation, textbooks, and health services, such funds to be disbursed independently of public educational authorities in those states that prohibited state funds for parochial schools. In this way the federal funds would go directly to the religious and non-public authorities. Neither bill passed the Senate.

In the eightieth Congress the same question came up again in substantially the same form. S472 followed the formula of S181 to allow the states to decide the use of federal funds for religious schools; whereas S717 would have allowed the federal government to by-pass state authorities and grant federal subsidies for non-instructional purposes directly to parochial schools wherever state law prohibited state funds for religious schools. Finally, in April 1948 bill S472 was passed by the Senate, the first bill for general federal aid to pass either house of Congress since the nineteenth century. The House, however, did not take action on federal aid in the eightieth Congress.

In the first session of the eighty-first Congress the Senate on May 5, 1949 by the overwhelming vote of 58 to 15 quickly passed S246, which followed the formula of S472, but when the question came up in House committee a violent religious controversy was set off. Hearings were held by the House Committee on Education and Labor, and then on June 7 the House Subcommittee on Federal Aid to Education reported favorably on HR4643 (the Barden bill) which provided for federal funds to be used for current expenditures of public schools only. It explicitly ruled out transportation and health services from the meaning of "current expenditures."

The press and Congress were flooded with letters and comments on both sides of the issue. Meanwhile, on August 1, 1949, a new bill was introduced (HR5838) which would require 10 per cent of the annual federal aid to be used for auxiliary services (transportation, textbooks, and health) to all school children, and in those states where public funds could not be legally used for parochial schools the federal government was to make the payments directly to the parochial and private schools. In the midst of the furor the House Committee on Education and Labor failed to report to the House. Thus the matter died with the end of the first session of the eighty-first Congress.

The drive for federal funds for parochial school children

seems to be trying to lump all auxiliary services together in one federal aid bill or defeat federal aid entirely if it does not include them. The Senate in the eighty-first Congress, however, began to take another road by separating health services from general aid to education. It passed S1411 to grant money to the states for health services to all school children, including parochial as well as public school children. This act, like the School Lunch Act,[30] would make it possible for such funds to be paid directly to parochial school agencies in those states where such payment is now prohibited by the states.

Those who approve health services for all children no matter what school they attend but who still wish to abide by the historic conception of separation of church and state see dangers in by-passing the state authorities. They argue that if health services are to be provided for parochial school children the control of such benefits should be completely in the hands of public health or other state authorities, and should not pass into the hands of the private and religious agencies themselves.

A policy that attempts to conform with the historic conception of separation as outlined in the foregoing chapters would appear to rest upon the following two principles:

1. Any "auxiliary service" that aids the child to receive instruction in religious schools should be considered as direct or indirect aid to the school itself and thus comes under the ban of the principle of separation of church and state. This policy would apply to the use of public funds for free transportation and free textbooks for parochial school children.

2. Any "auxiliary service" that is designed to protect and promote the public health and thus requires the state to follow *all* children no matter where they are should logically be under the direct control and supervision of public health authorities. Under this heading would come preventive medi-

cal and health services for the control of disease and epidemic and for health education and guidance. These services then would be in the hands of the public authorities in each state and administered by public health employees who themselves go to the children. Participation in such a program implies acceptance of professionally approved programs and standards of health education as well as medical and dental diagnosis and care.

This would put health services in a genuine "welfare" category apart from incidental school services. Thus health benefits would not be "auxiliary" services that aid the religious school indirectly to improve its facilities at public expense, but would be part of a welfare program that the state sees fit to provide for all children no matter where they attend school. This would be in harmony with the principle that public funds are to be spent only for programs that are managed and carried out by public officials in such ways that religious institutions are not supported, aided, or promoted directly or indirectly. On the basis of this distinction federal aid for health services to all children would be separated from provisions for general aid to the states for the improvement of their school systems. They belong in different categories.

There are indications that unless the rendering of "auxiliary services" to children in religious schools is reconsidered and unless health services are defined as above, the pressure will increase to define virtually every kind of educational activity as "auxiliary services" for the benefit of the child and thus constantly widen the use of public funds for aid to religious schools. Unless such limitations are made, the extent of "cooperation" or "entanglement" may well be indefinitely enlarged and the struggles of 175 years for separation of church and state effectively nullified. It is important that the issue as here involved should be clearly understood by the American people.

Another phase of the problem of aid to religious institutions is the question whether scholarships are to be provided by state or federal funds for qualified and needy students to aid them in attending secondary or higher institutions. The usual proposal is that recipients of such scholarships should be free to use the funds for attendance at institutions of their choice whether they be sectarian or public institutions. The model of the educational benefits for veterans (G. I. Bill of Rights) is usually quoted to support such use of scholarships. Two early court cases bear on the point. Both of them decided that tuition could not be paid from public funds to send students to sectarian institutions. One was a court case in South Dakota in 1891 (Dakota Synod v. State, 50 N. W. 632), and the other was in Kentucky in 1917, when it was declared that using public school funds to pay the tuition of high school pupils to attend a Presbyterian institution was unconstitutional:

. . . we may, with propriety, say in passing that the admitted arrangement between the board of education of Powell County and Stanton College, under which Stanton College was created a county high school and paid by the board of education out of the common school funds tuition fees for county high school pupils, is a flagrant violation of section 189 of the Constitution. . . .[31]

Decisions on large-scale, permanent programs of scholarships are complicated, but it may be that the pattern of the G. I. Bill should be re-examined to see if there is a difference between the use of public funds as special rewards to veterans for service to their country and the use of public funds on a continuing basis to grant scholarships that will undoubtedly aid sectarian institutions. The task for the public to decide is how to use public funds to aid worthy college students without discriminating on the basis of religion or creed and at the same time preserve the principle of separation which prohibits aid and support to sectarian institutions.

Use of Parochial Schools as Public Schools

Some of the foregoing practices can be highlighted in local community practices that illustrate the difficulties of close "co-operation" by church and state. A device that has become fairly common and that has given rise to bitter community feelings has been the practice of designating already established parochial schools to be used as public schools. This practice arises when public school facilities are inadequate or when a community fails to raise the funds to make adequate public schools available. The line of easiest resistance then may seem to be a simple one, namely, a community would decide not to go to the expense of taxation or bonds for new public school buildings but rather to pay rent or salaries or both to a parochial school and to send public school children to the parochial school for instruction. Sometimes the staff and instruction were changed but little if at all; in other cases the special religious instruction was not required of those public school children whose parents did not wish them to receive it. The National Education Association reported in 1946 that twenty-eight states had some form of this arrangement in effect.[32]

Since the First World War several court cases have arisen over this issue. Four of the most important ones have taken place in Kentucky, Iowa, Missouri, and New Mexico. They all decided that where sectarian teachers or sectarian instruction were involved, the practice was unconstitutional. In several other cases, where holding the public school in the church building did not seem to influence the children in any sectarian way, the practice was not prohibited. The difficult question to determine is always whether or not the plausible practice of using parochial school facilities because they are readily available is a result of religious opposition to the expansion of public school facilities. It would be easy for a community to refuse additional taxes or a bond issue for additional public schools, and then to argue that since the public school facilities are so limited it would be cheaper and easier to use religious schools than to build new public schools or to raise public school teachers' salaries.

Be that as it may, the quotations from the following court cases are illuminating:

In Kentucky the court ruled that:

The Constitution not only forbids the appropriation for any purpose or in any manner of the common school funds to sectarian or denominational institutions, but it contemplates that the separation between the common school and the sectarian or denominational school or institution shall be so open, notorious, and complete that there can be no room for reasonable doubt that the common school is absolutely free from the influence, control, or domination of the sectarian institution or school.[33]

The Iowa court said:

Every influence of association and environment, and of precept and example, to say nothing of authority, were thus contrived to keep those of Catholic parentage loyal to their faith and to bias in the same direction those of non-Catholic parentage. In short, so far as its immediate management and control were concerned, the manner of imparting instruction, both secular and religious, and the influence and leadership exercised over the minds of the pupils, it was as thoroughly and completely a religious parochial school as it could well have been had it continued in name as well as in practice the school of the parish under the special charge and supervision of the church, its clergy and religious orders. The act of the board in thus surrendering its proper functions and duties is not to be explained as a mere change in the location of the public school or a mere exercise of the discretion which the law gives to the board to rent a schoolroom when circumstances render it necessary. It was a practical elimination of the public school as such and a transfer of its name and its revenues to the upper department of the parochial school.[34]

The board of directors had no authority to clothe a religious school with the character of a public school. . . .[35]

. . . the state shall be watchful to forbid the use or abuse of any of its functions, powers, or privileges in the interest of any church or creed.

If there is any one thing which is well settled in the policies and purposes of the American people as a whole, it is the fixed and unalterable determination that there shall be an absolute and un-equivocal separation of church and state, and that our public school system, supported by the taxation of the property of all alike — Catholic, Protestant, Jew, Gentile, believer, and infidel — shall not be used, directly or indirectly, for religious instruction, and above all, that it shall not be made an instrumentality of proselyting in-fluence in favor of any religious organization, sect, creed, or belief. So well is this understood, it would be a waste of time for us, at this point, to stop for specific reference to authorities or precedents, or to the familiar pages of American history bearing thereon.[36]

The Missouri court stated:

It is apparent that under our system of education the inclusion of the St. Cecelia school in the public school system and its main-tenance as a part of and an adjunct to the parish church in its religious teaching, and where children of every faith may be com-pelled to attend and have attended, constitutes a denial of our guaranty of religious freedom; the fact that attendance at Mass is customarily before school hours or that religious instruction may be given during recess periods or that the participation of a non-Catholic child in these services may not be required does not make such conduct lawful in view of this provision.[37]

One of the most widely publicized and carefully investigated situations began in North College Hill, Ohio in 1940 and came to a bitter and violent climax in 1947. The circumstances here may have been little different from that in many other communities, but seldom have the facts been documented so well by field investigators who were invited to examine the situation carefully and to make recommendations.[38] The main purpose of the investigation was not to investigate the religious issue but to investigate the relations between the board of education and the superintendent of schools. In the interests of objectivity it is therefore desirable to quote extensively from the N. E. A. report itself. The background of the situation was as follows:

In 1939 North College Hill was a village of some five thousand inhabitants. Its school system was classified for administrative purposes, under the Ohio General Code, as an Exempted Village School District. The school board was composed of five elected members, three Protestants and two Catholics. In 1940 this board at a special meeting adopted a proposal under which the St. Margaret Mary parochial school was incorporated into the public school system, and was officially designated as Public School Number 3. This was effected through an arrangement under which the board of education leased the parochial school building for a two-year period and placed the teachers of the school on the payroll of the board of education. During the following school year it operated as a public school with no changes in teaching personnel or curriculum. This transfer seems to have aroused no apparent opposition immediately in the community. However, within a few months, certain non-Catholic elements began to object to the arrangement and started to organize for the 1941 board election.

Meanwhile, the 1940 census revealed that North College Hill was eligible to become a city and in 1941 was so incorporated. As a result, the school system ceased to be operated as an Exempted Village School District and became classified as a City School District. This necessitated the election of a new five-man school board.

During the 1941 election campaign, the most important local issue was the question of whether the former parochial school should continue to remain in the public school system. The campaign literature freely conceded this to be the issue and community opinion was split largely along sectarian lines. The election resulted in a new board consisting of four Protestants and one Catholic.

In February 1942 the new board voted to notify the St. Margaret Mary School authorities that the existing arrangements, due to expire in June 1942, would not be renewed for the coming school year. This action was presumably approved at the time by a majority of the voters who, in the biennial election of 1943, elected Protestants to the two board vacancies. In July of that year the then superintendent of schools had resigned and William A. Cook had been appointed.

In the fall of 1945, the regular biennial election was held to fill the vacancies of three members whose terms were expiring January 1, 1946. Again the candidates campaigned primarily on the parochial school issue, and again community support split largely along sectarian lines. It is clear, however, that a number of Catholic residents were opposed to the reincorporation of the parochial school into the public school system. It is likewise clear that a number of non-Catholics supported the reincorporation. The latter were persuaded in part at least by the argument that an additional number of students classified as public-school students would substantially increase the amount of state aid which the school system would receive.

The election took place in November and there is no question but that it was fairly conducted and that the issue was fully discussed. Three Catholics were elected to fill the vacancies for four-year terms, thereby gaining a three to two majority control of the board on the principal issue. This constituted the make-up of the board until June 17, 1947, when all members resigned.[39]

Thereupon the superintendent and the majority members of the board of education began to have difficulties over the right of the superintendent to recommend appointments and promotions for the teaching and administrative staff of the school system. The majority members of the board insisted that the superintendent recommend certain appointments and refused to accept any of his recommendations until he had submitted the records of candidates for the board's review. Finally, the majority of the board refused to reappoint the superintendent himself, whereupon most of the teachers in the system resigned in protest, the vast majority of students went on strike with their parents' approval, mass meetings were held, and mass petitions were circulated condemning the board's action and demanding the reinstatement of the superintendent:

By February of 1947 schoolboard meetings were being attended by anywhere from five hundred to a thousand people. It would be difficult to exaggerate the bitterness which was engendered. Feeling became so intense that the schoolboard meeting held on April

15 ended in a riot. Two majority members of the board were physically mistreated, one requiring medical attention. At the meeting scheduled in May, more than twenty policemen were in attendance.

Probably the most unfortunate consequence arising out of the North College Hill situation has been the marked spread of and increase in tension between certain members of the Catholic and Protestant faiths. Although the immediate focus of the dispute centered in the policies and conduct of the majority members of the board, the whole controversial question of the use of public funds in support of sectarian education has been brought into the open with attending widespread publicity.[40]

Here was a case where the entire school system of a whole community was disrupted over the religious issue. No better example could be given of the way the attempt of state and church to "co-operate" led to the strengthening of divisive forces in the community. This is but the continuation of the long history of the same divisiveness that has occurred whenever religious controversies have been injected into educational matters.

A still more recent example of similar practices and similar results took place in New Mexico and culminated in a widely publicized court case. This situation had its origin in Dixon, New Mexico and had its counterpart in several other New Mexico communities. This case vividly illustrates the combination of the whole range of "auxiliary services" described in the foregoing pages. Here, not only were 139 priests, nuns, and brothers found to be teachers in 27 parochial schools that received tax support and thus were used as public schools for all children, but also tax funds were used for bus transportation and free textbooks to parochial school children. This was apparently what the Roman Catholic Church in New Mexico felt was a desirable kind of "co-operation" between the church and a state in which Catholics were a majority.

This whole arrangement was declared unconstitutional and

was prohibited by District Court Judge E. T. Hensley on March 12, 1949. He decreed:

(1) That the following named defendants be and each are hereby declared to be forever barred from receiving any school moneys and employment in the public schools of this state, to-wit: [The names of 124 Catholic nuns, 13 brothers, and two priests follow.]

(2) That school students are subject to the supervision of school authorities and teachers from the time that they arrive at the school in the morning until they leave in the afternoon and this entire period of time is hereby adjudged and decreed and declared to be a part of the school day for all such children.

(3) That Section 17, Article 20 of the Constitution of the State of New Mexico requires that the members of the New Mexico State Board of Education adopt a uniform system of textbooks.

(4) That the adopting of sectarian indoctrinated textbooks and furnishing the same to the tax-supported schools of the State of New Mexico by the State of New Mexico or the members of the New Mexico State Board of Education violates Section 4, Article 21 of the Constitution of the State of New Mexico and the First Amendment to the Constitution of the United States as made applicable to the states by the Fourteenth Amendment to the Constitution of the United States.

(5) That the furnishing of free textbooks to schools other than tax-supported schools of this State, violates Section 14, Article 9 of the Constitution of the State of New Mexico and Section 3, Article 12, of the Constitution of the State of New Mexico.

(6) That the furnishing by the State of New Mexico of sectarian indoctrinated textbooks or textbooks for Catholic schools only to private parochial schools is in violation of the First Amendment to the Constitution of the United States.

(7) That the furnishing by the State of New Mexico of free school bus transportation to pupils of parochial schools is in violation of Section 3, Article 12 and Section 14, Article 9 of the Constitution of the State of New Mexico and the First Amendment to the Constitution of the United States

as made applicable to the states by the Fourteenth Amendment to the Constitution of the United States.

(8) That the teaching of sectarian doctrine in the tax-supported schools of this State violates Section 4, Article 21 of the Constitution of the State of New Mexico and Section 9, Article 12 of the Constitution of the State of New Mexico and the First Amendment to the Constitution of the United States as made applicable to the States by the Fourteenth Amendment to the Constitution of the United States.

(9) That the holding of tax-supported school classes in buildings which have religious emblems such as crosses, grottos, religious statuary and religious pictures, all peculiar to a certain denomination, violates the First Amendment to the Constitution of the United States as made applicable to the states by the Fourteenth Amendment to the Constitution of the United States.

(10) That the holding of tax-supported school classes in a building owned by the Roman Catholic Church or an Order thereof or an Official thereof, part of said building being retained by said Order, Church or Official for use as a private or parochial school is in violation of the First Amendment to the Constitution of the United States as made applicable to the states by the Fourteenth Amendment to the Constitution of the United States.

(11) It is hereby adjudged, decreed and declared that there is no separation between Church and State as contemplated and required by the First and Fourteenth Amendments to the Constitution of the United States in the following named schools, all in the State of New Mexico: [27 schools are listed.] [41]

Here is a thoroughgoing reliance upon the principle of separation of church and state. The judgment seems to be directly in line with the historical meaning of the principle of separation as defined in this book. It follows the reasoning of the minority opinion in the Everson case described earlier and accords with the McCollum decision to be described in some detail in the following pages.

SHALL SECTARIAN RELIGIOUS INSTRUCTION BE PROMOTED BY THE PUBLIC SCHOOLS?

The foregoing pages have shown that the question of public funds for religious schools today no longer concerns direct aid but has shifted to the problem of indirect aid through "auxiliary services." The second proposition (cited at the beginning of this chapter) involving the principle of separation in education has also taken a somewhat different form since 1900. With respect to the issue of religious instruction in public schools the general practice is no longer to require all children to be taught the specific sectarian doctrines of a single religion as a part of the public school curriculum. With such exceptions as just noted in New Mexico, public schools do not ordinarily teach the doctrines, the catechism, or the prayer book of Episcopalians, or Presbyterians, or Congregationalists, or Roman Catholics. That has been legally prohibited by the first 125 years of our constitutional history. But since 1900, and especially since the First World War, the demand has grown insistently that some forms of religious instruction should be given in the public schools. The most common forms of this demand include a re-emphasis upon Bible reading in public school classrooms and a new emphasis upon released time for sectarian religious instruction.

Those who defend Bible reading in the public schools argue that the Bible is the depository of the common moral and ethical traditions of the Western world upon which our civilization is based and that therefore it should be read to all children in the public schools. They argue that if the Bible is read without comment and without interpretation by the teacher it is not a sectarian religious book and thus does no violence to anyone's religious beliefs. On this basis and under the pressure principally of Protestant groups several states have passed laws requiring or permitting the reading of the Bible without comment.

Opponents of Bible reading argue that since the King James version of the Bible is the one most commonly used it is definitely a Protestant religious book. It is therefore sectarian in the eyes of Jews, other non-Christians, and Roman Catholics. They hold that its reading is therefore a violation of the equal rights of conscience. The courts have been divided on this issue, but most courts have decided that Bible reading, if read with no comment, is permissible even in states where the constitutions or statutes prohibit sectarian instruction in the public schools.

In recent years, and especially since the beginning of the Second World War, another emphasis upon religious instruction has been achieved through the practice of excusing pupils during school hours to attend religious instruction given by their own religious instructors, either within or outside the public school buildings. This device, the so-called practice of "released time," arose because certain religious groups were dissatisfied with the limited amount of religious instruction that could be achieved through Bible reading, a limitation that the principle of separation had imposed upon the earlier practice of direct sectarian instruction in the public schools.

Proponents of released time argue that the public schools have become godless and secular in their impact upon children and that the neglect of the great moral resources to be obtained in religious instruction has led to a lessening of sound morals and the alarming growth of juvenile delinquency. They argue that the churches cannot achieve their aims in an hour or two a week on Sunday and that therefore the public schools should "co-operate" with the churches in promoting and making possible religious instruction that will promote the moral welfare of all. Several states have passed permissive legislation allowing released time programs, and the court cases have again been divided as to the constitutionality of such programs.

Opponents of released time maintain that religious instruction is the domain of the parents and churches through their own agencies and by their own voluntary efforts. They argue that religious groups should redouble their efforts as they see fit among their own constituencies but should not use the machinery or enforcing power of the state through its public schools to foster or aid religious groups in these efforts. To do so is to use tax funds or the influence of the state in promoting religion in violation of the principle of separation of church and state and the principle of equal rights of conscience. To anyone who may not find his own specific religious belief represented in a program of released time religious instruction conducted during public school hours, such a practice appears to be a multiple establishment of religion in violation of his rights of conscience.

Thus the controversy goes back and forth with respect to religious instruction in public schools. The issue has increased in public concern and emotional intensity. What the American people must decide is, again, whether the historic principle of separation of church and state prohibits this indirect promotion of religious instruction as clearly as it prohibits direct sectarian instruction. Is Bible reading sectarian instruction? If so, it is prohibited by the principle of separation. Is Bible reading non-sectarian religious instruction? If it is, does it come under the ban of multiple establishment of religion? If the American people wish to adhere to the principle of separation as seen in the long perspective of history, they should decide to prohibit non-sectarian religious instruction in public schools as a form of multiple establishment of religion.

Is released time a form of impartial encouragement of religion by the state? If so, it too becomes a form of multiple establishment of religion with all the dangers of "co-operation" or "entanglement" that have been found to be present in the efforts of the past to promote religion through the public school system. The line where "co-operation" becomes fusion of church and state is difficult to define.

Such questions and answers as these may seem to be harsh to some people of good will and genuine religious motivation, but the logic of the historical considerations for sound public policy seems clear to those who have the best interests of religion and of public education at heart. There is no easy answer to these problems in a nation of divided religious loyalties, but the consequences of religious strife in the past seem to indicate that the road of wisdom for America is toward less intermixture between church and state rather than more. Where the road to "co-operation" becomes "entanglement" has always been the critical question. The better part of wisdom is for church and state to take separate roads. When highways are too narrow for heavy traffic, congestions or accidents are bound to occur. Divided lanes enable different kinds of vehicles to proceed safely at appropriate speeds in the same direction. Highways that provide adequate safety barriers promote the smooth flow of traffic when it is moving in different directions, and highways with overpasses and underpasses prevent accidents where traffic intersects. Sound public policy should be devoted to the prevention of "tie-ups" and "accidents" between church and state in education. Some of the ways in which church and state tend to tangle or collide over these issues are illustrated below.

Bible Reading

Public decisions on the wisdom and constitutionality of Bible reading in the public schools are made exceedingly difficult because of the contradictory positions taken by state constitutions, state legislation, and court decisions. Some of these contradictions are summarized here.[42]

The constitutions of twelve states specifically prohibit sectarian instruction in the public schools. These states are Arizona, California, Colorado, Idaho, Minnesota, Montana, Nebraska, Nevada, New York, South Dakota, Wisconsin, and Wyoming. Typical of these prohibitions is the Wyoming Constitution of 1889:

> No sectarian instruction, qualifications or tests shall be imparted, exacted, applied or in any manner tolerated in the schools of any grade or character controlled by the State, nor shall attendance be required at any religious service therein, nor shall any sectarian tenets or doctrines be taught or favored in any public school or institution that may be established under this constitution.[43]

No state constitution explicitly prohibits the reading of the Bible as such, and therefore the decision as to whether Bible reading is or is not sectarian instruction has been left to the courts. The Constitution of Mississippi explicitly states that the rights of religious liberty do not exclude the Holy Bible from use in any public school in the state.

The state laws are much more confusing than the constitutional provisions. Twenty-four states have passed laws prohibiting sectarian instruction in the public schools. These are Arizona, California, Delaware, Idaho, Georgia, Indiana, Kansas, Kentucky, Maine, Maryland, Mississippi, Massachusetts, Montana, Nevada, New Hampshire, New Jersey, New Mexico, North Dakota, Oklahoma, South Carolina, South Dakota, Utah, Wisconsin, and Washington. Here is a clear statement of the general principle in half of the states.

Most of these states, however, do not interpret Bible reading as sectarian instruction. Twelve states have passed laws *requiring* that the Bible be read in the public schools. Seven of these twelve also have laws prohibiting sectarian instruction. (These seven are Delaware, Georgia, Idaho, Kentucky, Maine, Massachusetts, and New Jersey.) The other five states that require Bible reading are Alabama, Arkansas, Florida, Pennsylvania, and Tennessee. All except Massachusetts have passed their laws since 1913.

In addition to the above there are six states that permit Bible reading in the public schools, despite general statutory prohibition against sectarian instruction. In addition, Idaho has a constitutional prohibition against sectarian instruction. Nine of the eighteen provide that no comment shall accompany the reading of the Bible, and seven provide that children who object to listening may be excused from the exercises. These protections are thought sufficient to provide for freedom of religious conscience of minority groups.

The spread of custom and actual practice on Bible reading is indicated by a survey conducted by the National Education Association.[44] State superintendents reported that not only was Bible reading required by law in twelve states but it was permitted in twenty-five other states either by law, by interpretation of courts, by attorney general ruling, by state department of education ruling, or by local custom. Superintendents in eight states reported that it was not done (Arizona, California, Illinois, Louisiana, New York, South Dakota, Washington, and Wisconsin), and three did not answer (Minnesota, Montana, and Nevada). This makes a total of thirty-seven states that require or permit Bible reading. Much of this practice results from court decisions that have so interpreted state constitutions.

Large numbers of cases on the legality of Bible reading have been tried since 1900, and most courts have ruled that Bible reading is not unconstitutional and thus is permissible if no comment is added and if pupils who object are excused from participating. Many of the cases ruled that the decision should be left to local authorities.[45] Many of the cases also called forth vigorous dissents from judges who believed that the majority opinions violated constitutional provisions against compulsory support of religious teachings and violated guarantees of freedom of religious conscience.

Typical of the decisions upholding the constitutionality of required Bible reading and prayers is that of the Georgia supreme court in 1921. The court argued that the reading of the Bible does not give offense to Roman Catholic or Jewish pupils:

It would require a strained and unreasonable construction to find anything in the ordinance which interferes with the natural and inalienable right to worship God according to the dictates of one's own conscience. The mere listening to the reading of an extract from the Bible and a brief prayer at the opening of school exercises would seem far remote from such interference.[46]

The majority opinion in this case further argued that complete separation of church and state had never been intended by the founders of the state and thus recognized that Bible reading was a form of "co-operation."

The dissent in the Georgia case argued that the King James version of the Bible *does* offend the religious convictions of Roman Catholics, Jews, and some Protestants as well as deists, agnostics, and atheists:

. . . making the reading of the King James version of the Bible a part of the worship of the public schools puts municipal approval upon the version, and thus discriminates in favor of and aids the Protestant sects of the Christian religion.[47]

Typical of minority decisions in cases where Bible reading has been upheld were those in Michigan and Minnesota. The Michigan dissent said:

If their position is sound, not only should the Bible be taught, but all other forms of Christian religious instruction should be given in the schools. If this reasoning is sound, the constitution left it open to the school authorities to determine what variety of Christian religion they should teach, and the school board of the city of Detroit has the power today to have taught in the public schools of the city of Detroit the theological tenets of any Christian church.[48]

In the Minnesota dissent the minority developed an argument that is directly in line with Madison's conception of the equal rights of conscience as superior to toleration of religious beliefs:

The Constitution not only says that every man may "worship God according to the dictates of his own conscience," but it says:
"Nor shall any control of or interference with the rights of conscience be permitted."
"Rights of conscience" means what? By conscience we mean that internal conviction or self-knowledge that tells us that a thing is right or wrong. It is that faculty or power within us which decides on the right or wrong of an act and approves or condemns. It is our moral sense which dictates to us right or wrong. Each person is governed by his own views. The "rights of conscience," in religious matters, means the privilege of resting in peace or contentment according to one's own judgment. It is a recognition of a right to religious complacency. . . .
To require the Jewish children to read the New Testament which extols Christ as the Messiah is to tell them that their religious teachings at home are untrue. . . .
The Catholic people do not believe it right to have a Bible read to their children in the absence of the light of construction placed thereon by their church. Are these people to be content to have a Bible read which substantially ignores the doctrine of purgatory, which is one of their vital beliefs? On the contrary, may a Catholic school board have the Catholic version of the Bible read disclosing the theory of purgatory as indicated in the Book of Maccabees, and not interfere with the "rights of conscience" of Protestants . . . ?
No man must feel that his religion is tolerated. His constitutional "rights of conscience" should be indefeasible and beyond the control or interference of men. The constitution says so. . . .
No decision pro or con has thoroughly considered the construction of the specific language:
"Nor shall any control of or interference with the rights of conscience be permitted."
We have an opportunity here to construe this language. The majority opinion has ignored it. It should be construed in accordance with the best interests of the people. This permits but one conclusion.[46]

In at least five states the majority opinions took a position that prohibited Bible reading in the public schools on grounds directly in line with the minority opinions outlined above. These decisions were in Wisconsin, Illinois, Louisiana, South Dakota, and Washington.

The unanimous decision in Wisconsin argued that equality of religious conscience is the only sound basis for deciding the issue:

> When we remember that wise and good men have struggled and agonized through the centuries to find the correct interpretation of the scriptures, employing to that end all the resources of great intellectual power, profound scholarship, and exalted spiritual attainment, and yet with such widely divergent results; and, further, that the relators conscientiously believe that their church furnishes them means, and the only means, of correct and infallible interpretation,—we can scarcely say their conscientious scruples against the reading of any version of the Bible to their children, unaccompanied by such interpretation, are entitled to no consideration.[50]

The Illinois decision in 1910 held that the Bible was a sectarian book and thus its reading discriminated against Catholics and non-Christians and that the public school, like the government, must be secular in its aims:

> The Bible, in its entirety is a sectarian book as to the Jew and every believer in any religion other than the Christian religion, and as to those who are heretical or who hold beliefs that are not regarded as orthodox. Whether it may be called sectarian or not, its use in the schools necessarily results in sectarian instruction. There are many sects of Christians, and their differences grow out of their differing constructions of various parts of the Scriptures — the different conclusions drawn as to the effect of the same words.[51]
>
> It is true that this is a Christian state. The great majority of its people adhere to the Christian religion. No doubt this is a Protestant state. The majority of its people adhere to one or another of the Protestant denominations. But the law knows no distinction between the Christian and the Pagan, the Protestant and the Catholic. All are citizens. Their civil rights are precisely equal. . . . The school, like the government, is simply a civil institution. It is secular and not religious in its purposes. The truths of the

Bible are the truths of religion, which do not come within the province of the public school.[52]

It is interesting to note that many of the cases brought to trial to prohibit Bible reading were brought on behalf of Roman Catholic plaintiffs and in some cases on behalf of Jewish plaintiffs. In all cases involving Catholic parents it was argued that Bible reading from the King James version and without comment was actually Protestant sectarianism and thus violated the rights of conscience of Catholic children. It is evident that Protestant groups and the Protestant outlook have been the great impetus behind the movement for Bible reading and that the fundamental outlook of judges who affirmed its constitutionality has conformed to the Protestant assumptions that the Bible is the common religious and moral heritage of all Americans.

In the light of the long historical meaning of separation of church and state it seems clear that Protestant Bible reading might well be construed as a multiple establishment of religion or that it is intended to give state support and sanction to the religious beliefs of Protestants in general in preference to those of Roman Catholics, Jews, other non-Christians, and non-believers.

When the religious communities are so much divided concerning their interpretations of the Bible it seems the better part of wisdom for the civil courts not to try to interpret the religious doctrines of the Bible for them. When a civil court attempts to do so, it surely comes close to setting itself up as "a competent Judge of Religious truth" or as employing "Religion as an engine of Civil policy" (Madison's words in his *Memorial and Remonstrance*). The historical evidence suggests that the public welfare is better served when the state does not try to define the religious convictions of individuals either by legislation or court action, but rather assumes the equal rights of all to believe or not to believe according to their consciences.

Where reasonable doubt exists concerning religious practices in the public schools, the test of the principle of separation
would indicate that the less the state attempts to promote
religion through its public schools the better. Otherwise, the
state will inevitably make invidious distinctions among varying religious beliefs or will assume that the religious rights of
minorities are to be considered more lightly than are the religious opinions of the majority. The safer assumption is that
the state has no competent role in deciding matters of religious
faith.

Public School Teachers in Religious Garb

Much less extensive than Bible reading, but nevertheless
the cause of considerable controversy where it has occurred,
is the practice of permitting public school teachers to perform
their duties in religious dress. Again the practice has varied
and court decisions have been diametrically opposed.

In a Pennsylvania decision in 1894 the majority ruled that
the wearing of religious garb and insignia by members of
the Sisters of Charity did not constitute sectarian teaching and
that to exclude them from teaching in the public schools would
violate their rights of religious freedom. The dissent argued
that such apparel *was* sectarian in its influence. Thereupon
the state legislature passed a law prohibiting the wearing of
religious dress in the public schools, and this law was held
to be constitutional in 1910 when the court decided that the
state had the right to determine the qualifications of its teachers and to set reasonable regulations for their conduct.

We cannot assent to the proposition that the intent or the effect
of the legislation is to disqualify any person from employment as a
teacher "on account of his religious sentiments." It is directed
against acts, not beliefs, and only against acts of the teacher while
engaged in the performance of his or her duties as such teacher.[58]

The system of common school education in this commonwealth
is the creature of the state, and its perpetuity and freedom from

sectarian control are guaranteed by express constitutional provisions. Subject to these, the power to support and maintain an efficient system of public schools, wherein all the children of the commonwealth above the age of six years may be educated, is vested in the legislature. This carries with it the authority to determine what shall be the qualifications of the teachers, but in prescribing them the legislature may not make religious belief or church affiliation a test. Nevertheless, the power of the legislature to make reasonable regulations for the government of their conduct while engaged in the performance of their duties must be conceded. Primarily it is the province of the legislature to determine what regulations will promote the efficiency of the system and tend to the accomplishment of the object for which it was established. It is only where such regulations are clearly shown to be in violation of the fundamental law that the courts, even though entertaining a different opinion from that of the legislature as to the necessity for or the wisdom or expedience of adopting them, may annul them.[54]

The highest court in New York in 1906 ruled that teachers in religious garb could be excluded from the public schools because such garb exerted a sectarian influence:

Here we have the plainest possible declaration of the public policy of the state as opposed to the prevalence of sectarian influences in the public schools. . . . There can be little doubt that the effect of the costume worn by these Sisters of St. Joseph at all times in the presence of their pupils would be to inspire respect if not sympathy for the religious denomination to which they so manifestly belong. To this extent the influence was sectarian, even if it did not amount to the teaching of denominational doctrine.[55]

A recent controversy on this particular issue on a state-wide basis took place in North Dakota. The state supreme court had held in 1936 that the wearing of religious dress did not violate the constitution of North Dakota, but in July 1948 the people of North Dakota adopted a referendum prohibiting teachers in public schools from wearing religious garb denoting a religious order or denomination. Arizona, Nebraska, and Oregon have also passed laws forbidding religious garb in the public schools, but these laws have not been tested in the courts. The bearings on this issue of the controversies in North College Hill, Ohio and in New Mexico have already been discussed in another connection.

The trend here is plain. At first the courts said that the wearing of religious dress was permissible, but by laws, referendum, and by state department of education ruling, such practice has been prohibited, and the courts have upheld these measures. This policy seems to be in line with the historic principle of separation as described in these pages.

Released Time

The most widely publicized kind of religious instruction in recent years has taken the form of released time. A wide variety of practices is employed, but in general those children whose parents so desire are released from their regular public school classes for a certain period of time each week in order that they may go to their churches or synagogues or in order that religious teachers may come to the public school buildings to give specific religious instruction to the children. The practice has spread so rapidly that in 1947 the International Council of Religious Education claimed that 2,000,000 public school children were enrolled in released time classes in 2200 communities.

These figures may or may not accurately represent the actual state of affairs, but at least sixteen states have passed permissive laws regarding released time and at least thirty-three state superintendents in 1946 reported to the National Education Association that the practice was permitted in their states. The practice gained headway in the 1920's, spread in the 1930's, and increased rapidly in the 1940's.

More recent studies of the extent of released time practices seem to indicate that the programs may be less widely in force than the earlier claims indicated. The Research Division of the National Education Association made a wide canvass in

December 1948 by sending questionnaires to 5100 local superintendents of schools. On the basis of 2639 replies it was found that 61 per cent of the school systems (a total of 1621 communities) reported that no plan of released time had ever been in effect, 12 per cent (310 communities) reported that their programs had been given up, and 27 per cent (708 communities) reported that some kind of plan was in effect.[56] Thus about three-fourths of these school systems had no plan of released time in operation. A much higher proportion (46 per cent) of the larger cities had programs than did the smaller towns. On the basis of this study the N.E.A. Research Division estimated that about 700,000 elementary and secondary school pupils were enrolled in released time programs in 1948-49. Inasmuch as only about half the superintendents replied to the questionnaire it is possible that the total number of students enrolled in released time programs in the country might reach anywhere from 1,500,000 to 2,000,000.

Court decisions on the constitutionality of released time have been divided. A New York court ruled out the practice in Mount Vernon in 1925, and another court in 1927 passed favorably upon it as instituted in White Plains. When put together these decisions reflect an interesting conflict of opinion. With respect to Mount Vernon the court said:

The fact that no particular denomination was favored or intended so to be by this action of the board of education does not affect the question. . . .

I find nothing whatsoever in the Education Law authorizing either the board of education, the state commissioner of education, or the education department to change, limit, or shorten the time of attendance. . . .

Education Law . . . prescribes the instruction required in public schools. Religious instruction is not one of them. Consequently it would be unlawful and unauthorized for a board of education to substitute religious instruction in the school in place of the instruction required. To permit the pupils to leave the school during school hours for religious instruction would accomplish the same purpose, and would in effect substitute religious instruction for the instruction required by law.[57]

The opposite outlook was shown in the White Plains decision:

It is natural that parents should wish their children to have religious instruction at any favorable opportunity. It is not thought wise that it should be given directly in the school. But, when children are assembled, they may be sent elsewhere. We are told that in 23 other states there are in force methods similar to those employed here. . . . They [the commissioner and the local authorities] recognize that all education is not acquired in the schools; that, except for subjects legally prescribed, the parents may select the studies their children shall pursue; that it is the right of parents to direct the destiny of their children and guide them along paths of filial duty, as well as in those of obligation to the state . . . and that a belief in religion is not foreign to our system of government.[58]

In 1940 New York state passed a law permitting local boards of education to institute the practice if they wished, and a comprehensive program was begun in New York City in February 1941.

Court cases in California and Illinois in 1947 continued the process of permitting released time, and the trend seemed to be accelerating especially under the leadership of Protestant and Catholic groups. When the Illinois case was appealed to the United States Supreme Court, however, the trend was reversed, for the court ruled on March 8, 1948 in the McCollum case that the program of released time in Champaign, Illinois was unconstitutional under the First Amendment as made applicable to the states through the Fourteenth Amendment.

The most significant arguments in the majority opinion of the McCollum case, written by Mr. Justice Black, were as follows:

The foregoing facts, without reference to others that appear in the record, show the use of tax-supported property for religious instruction and the close cooperation between the school authorities and the religious council in promoting religious education. The operation of the State's compulsory education system thus assists and is integrated with the program of religious instruction carried on by separate religious sects. Pupils compelled by law to go to school for secular education are released in part from their legal duty upon the condition that they attend the religious classes. *This is beyond all question a utilization of the tax-established and tax-supported public school system to aid religious groups to spread their faith. And it falls squarely under the ban of the First Amendment* (made applicable to the States by the Fourteenth) *as we interpreted it in Everson v. Board of Education,* 330 U. S. 1.[59]

To hold that a state cannot consistently with the First and Fourteenth Amendments utilize its public school system to aid any or all religious faiths or sects in the dissemination of their doctrines and ideals does not, as counsel urge, manifest a governmental hostility to religion or religious teachings. A manifestation of such hostility would be at war with our national tradition as embodied in the First Amendment's guaranty of the free exercise of religion. For the First Amendment rests upon the premise that both religion and government can best work to achieve their lofty aims if each is left free from the other within its respective sphere. Or, as we said in the *Everson* case, the First Amendment has erected a wall between Church and State which must be kept high and impregnable.

Here not only are the State's tax-supported public school buildings used for the dissemination of religious doctrines. The State also affords sectarian groups an invaluable aid in that it helps to provide pupils for their religious classes through use of the State's compulsory public school machinery. This is not separation of Church and State.[60]

The McCollum case raised a storm of protest from some Protestant and Catholic groups alike on the grounds that the Court had misinterpreted the meaning of the First Amendment and had promulgated a false conception of the historical meaning of separation of church and state. Much confusion arose as to whether specific programs of released time with their varying details of practice were or were not in violation of the supreme court ruling. Many groups decided to adopt a "wait and see" attitude. Indeed, in February 1949 the International Council of Religious Education announced that less than 10 per cent of weekday church school classes had stopped functioning as a result of the McCollum decision. Released time as a matter of public policy remained in doubt, but the evidence presented in this book indicates that the decision was based upon a sound historical interpretation of the meaning of separation of church and state. A clear understanding of the history involved ought to help to dispel confusion and doubt on this score.

In a separate concurring opinion written by Mr. Justice Frankfurter the conception of the role of the public school system in a religiously divided community was asserted with faithfulness to the historic principle of separation of church and state as follows:

> We are all agreed that the First and the Fourteenth Amendments have a secular reach far more penetrating in the conduct of Government than merely to forbid an "established church."[61]
>
> It is pertinent to remind that the establishment of this principle of Separation in the field of education was not due to any decline in the religious beliefs of the people. Horace Mann was a devout Christian, and the deep religious feeling of James Madison is stamped upon the Remonstrance. The secular public school did not imply indifference to the basic role of religion in the life of the people, nor rejection of religious education as a means of fostering it. The claims of religion were not minimized by refusing to make the public schools agencies for their assertion. The non-sectarian or secular public school was the means of reconciling freedom in general with religious freedom. The sharp confinement of the public schools to secular education was a recognition of the need of a democratic society to educate its children, in so far as the State undertook to do so, in an atmosphere free from pressures in a realm in which pressures are most resisted and where conflicts are most easily and most bitterly engendered. *Designed to serve as perhaps the most powerful agency for promoting cohesion among a heterogeneous democratic people, the public school must keep scrupulously free from entanglement in the strife of sects.* The preservation of the community from divisive conflicts, of Government from irreconcilable pressures by religious groups, of

religion from censorship and coercion however subtly exercised, requires strict confinement of the State to instruction other than religious, leaving to the individual's church and home, indoctrination in the faith of his choice.

This development of the public school as a symbol of our secular unity was not a sudden achievement nor attained without violent conflict. While in small communities of comparatively homogeneous religious beliefs, the need for absolute separation presented no urgencies, elsewhere the growth of the secular school encountered the resistance of feeling strongly engaged against it. But the inevitability of such attempts is the very reason for Constitutional provisions primarily concerned with the protection of minority groups. And such sects are shifting groups, varying from time to time, and place to place, thus representing in their totality the common interest of the nation.[62]

Religious education so conducted on school time and property is patently woven into the working scheme of the school. The Champaign arrangement thus presents powerful elements of inherent pressure by the school system in the interest of religious sects. The fact that this power has not been used to discriminate is beside the point. *Separation is a requirement to abstain from fusing functions of Government and of religious sects, not merely to treat them all equally.* That a child is offered an alternative may reduce the constraint; it does not eliminate the operation of influence by the school in matters sacred to conscience and outside the school's domain. The law of imitation operates, and nonconformity is not an outstanding characteristic of children. The result is an obvious pressure upon children to attend. Again, while the Champaign school population represents only a fraction of the more than two hundred and fifty sects of the nation, not even all the practicing sects in Champaign are willing or able to provide religious instruction. The children belonging to these nonparticipating sects will thus have inculcated in them a feeling of separatism when *the school should be the training ground for habits of community,* or they will have religious instruction in a faith which is not that of their parents. As a result, the public school system of Champaign actively furthers inculcation in the religious tenets of some faiths, and in the process sharpens the consciousness of religious differences at least among some of the children committed to its care. These are consequences not amenable to statistics. But they are precisely the consequences against which the Constitution was directed when it prohibited the Government common to all from becoming embroiled, however innocently, in the destructive religious conflicts of which the history of even this country records some dark pages.[63]

Separation means separation, not something less. Jefferson's metaphor in describing the relation between Church and State speaks of a "wall of separation," not of a fine line easily overstepped. *The public school is at once the symbol of our democracy and the most pervasive means for promoting our common destiny.* In no activity of the State is it more vital to keep out divisive forces than in its schools, to avoid confusing, not to say fusing, what the Constitution sought to keep strictly apart. "The great American principle of eternal separation" — Elihu Root's phrase bears repetition — is one of the vital reliances of our Constitutional system for assuring unities among our people stronger than our diversities. It is the Court's duty to enforce this principle in its full integrity.

We renew our conviction that "we have staked the very existence of our country on the faith that complete separation between the state and religion is best for the state and best for religion." *Everson v. Board of Education,* 330 U. S. at 59. If nowhere else, in the relation between Church and State, "good fences make good neighbors."[64]

When the outlooks of the two concurring opinions are combined, they represented eight of the nine supreme court justices, and they not only clearly interpreted the historic meaning of separation accurately but they also made a logical application to the practice of released time. If "establishment of religion" means only preference for a single church or religion, then released time may be appropriate to our history, but if separation of church and state also means prohibition of multiple establishment, as history clearly indicates, then the eight supreme court justices in the McCollum case enunciated principles that constitute the basis for sound public policy if the public wishes to hold to that historic principle.

Despite the Supreme Court's decision in the McCollum case, the controversy continues in demands made upon local boards of education and state legislatures for the continuation or initiation of released time programs. Similarly, court cases continue to be brought to prohibit released time programs. In 1948 a court in New York ruled that the system of released time in New York City was not prohibited by the McCollum case. The court found that the New York system was different from that in Champaign where public school buildings were used, whereas in New York the children left the public school buildings in order to receive religious instruction. The court argued that the McCollum case did not prohibit all released time programs as such, but that each program must be judged in the light of its own special arrangements. On this basis the court held that the New York system was free from the objectionable features of the Champaign program:

A reading of the several opinions in the McCollum case leads to a contrary conclusion, namely, that the constitutionality of a released time program is to be tested by a consideration of the factual aspects of the particular program under scrutiny.[65]

It thus appears that at least five of the nine Justices of the United States Supreme Court were in agreement upon the proposition that "Released Time" as such is not unconstitutional. . . . Furthermore, a reading of the entire opinion of Mr. Justice Black, who wrote for the Court in the McCollum case, seems reasonably subject to the interpretation that even he had no intention of passing in blanket terms upon the abstract issue of "Released Time" in general.[66]

In view of the opinion herein expressed that the decision in the McCollum case, supra, does not make "Released Time" as such unconstitutional, the programs challenged in this proceeding can only be condemned upon a finding that they are in aid of religion. That is the ground upon which the decision in the McCollum case is predicated. This court cannot so find. It believes the New York plan free from the objectionable features which motivated the United States Supreme Court to declare the Champaign plan unconstitutional.[67]

Fundamental is the right of the parent to rear his child in a particular religious faith, or to rear him as a non-believer if he so elects. Denial of this fundamental right to the parents now exercising the same through the medium of the New York released time programs should certainly not be made on speculative grounds.

Clearness and certainty are the factors that must control. Judged in the light of those essential requirements, this court can neither in law nor in conscience hold that the programs here assailed are constitutionally condemned by the McCollum decision.[68]

However, a district court in St. Louis in 1948 prohibited the continuance of the St. Louis released time program where public school buildings were not used. The court held that the differences between St. Louis and Champaign were inconsequential and argued that the McCollum decision was controlling in both cases, because the public schools were being used to aid sectarian groups to disseminate their doctrines:

The question before the Court is whether the program of religious instruction now in force in our public schools violates the Constitutional principle requiring separation of church and state.

In the recent case of People of the State of Illinois ex rel. McCollum v. Board of Education of Champaign County, Illinois (68 U.S. Supr. Ct. Rep., 461), the Supreme Court of the United States rules that the religious instruction program in Champaign county public schools violated this Constitutional provision. The essential facts in the instant case are substantially the same as in the McCollum case, and that decision is controlling here. In each case the party suing is a taxpayer, citizen, and parent of a child enrolled in the public schools. Both in Illinois and Missouri parents are required by law to send their children to the tax supported public schools (unless attending a private or a parochial school), there to remain in attendance during the entire time school is in session. The Champaign program permitted teachers employed by private religious groups, but subject to supervision by the superintendent of schools, to give religious instruction during school time in public school buildings to pupils whose parents had signed requests therefor; those children not attending such religious classes continuing their secular studies. The United States Supreme Court held that this program violated the Constitutional principle of church and state separation.

Our St. Louis system as now conducted differs from the Champaign system in that classes in religious instruction are not held in school buildings, school authorities neither exercise supervision over the teachers nor require them to keep attendance records and the school keeps none, and there is no limitation on sects entitled to participate in this program.

These differences are inconsequential. The controlling fact in both cases is that the public schools are used to aid sectarian groups to disseminate their doctrines. Whether these sectarian classes are conducted in the school buildings or elsewhere can make no difference, since attendance upon them during compulsory school hours is deemed attendance at school. Failure to exercise supervision over the instructors of religion and to require the keeping of proper attendance records does not make the school program legal; it merely indicates laxity on the part of the school authorities. The fact that any sect may participate in this program is immaterial; the public schools cannot be used to aid one religion or to aid all religions.

Perceiving no difference in principle between the program condemned in the McCollum case and the program in the instant case, the Court holds that the system of religious instruction as now conducted in our public school contravenes the First Amendment to our Constitution.

The violation of a citizen's constitutional rights is not compensable in damages, and one whose rights are thus invaded is entitled to prompt injunctive relief. The application for a temporary injunction will, therefore, be sustained.[69]

It is interesting to note that the St. Louis court used the argument that public schools could not be used to aid all religions any more than they could be used to aid one religion exclusively. This position is in line with the historical evidence that "establishment of religion" means multiple as well as single establishment. By the historical test, the St. Louis decision seems to rest upon sounder grounds than does the New York decision.

As the controversies continue, the courts and the public will do well to apply to each new instance the test of historical judgment as well as the test of sound practice based upon a democratic conception of the wise and the desirable.

SUMMARY OF HISTORICAL CONSIDERATIONS

This final chapter has noted some of the ways in which education has become the battleground between church and state in the first half of the twentieth century. The main lines of the controversy have been indicated along with some of the issues that will probably continue to be in the forefront of public decision in the years to come. The merits of specific instances have not been dealt with in detail, for many books, pamphlets, and articles have dealt with these issues in recent years from various points of view.[70] The purpose here has been to set forth the historical evidence that is fundamental to sound public policy. The history may then be used as one test, along with others, by which to determine whether any particular educational proposal conforms with or departs from the traditional meaning of separation of church and state.

In summary, then, the following conclusions may be drawn from the study of history concerning the meaning of the principle of separation of church and state for education in the United States:

(1) "Establishment of religion" historically meant multiple establishment as well as single establishment. The multiple meaning of establishment was widely recognized in the period of the late eighteenth century in America when the federal and early state constitutions were being formulated.

(2) Multiple as well as single establishment was prohibited by the First Amendment and by a majority of the original states prior to 1791.

(3) Multiple as well as single establishment was prohibited by virtually all of the original constitutions of those states that were added to the Union after 1791 and ultimately by all states either by constitution or by statute.

(4) The prohibition of "an establishment of religion" requires the state to be neutral toward all churches and all religions. The state may not "co-operate" with many religious groups any more than it may "co-operate" with a single preferred church. Whether one or many churches are involved, the "co-operation" becomes an alliance between church and state.

(5) Direct aid by federal or state governments to religious groups or religious institutions is "an establishment of religion" and thus unconstitutional. Direct aid or support to religious schools is aid to a religious institution and thus unconstitutional.

(6) Indirect financial or legal aid to religious agencies is likewise "an establishment of religion" and thus is unconstitutional.

(7) The principle of separation of church and state in education prohibits the use of public funds for many kinds of religious schools as fully as it prohibits the use of public funds for a single kind of sectarian school. It prohibits indirect aid through free transportation, free textbooks, and the like just as fully as it prohibits direct aid for constructing or maintaining religious school buildings or paying the salaries of religious teachers. "Auxiliary services" to children are indirect aids to the schools they attend.

(8) The principle of separation similarly (a) prohibits the promotion of a single sectarian religion, (b) prohibits "non-sectarian" religious instruction as embodied in Bible reading, and (c) prohibits the "impartial" promotion of many kinds of sectarian instruction as embodied in released time practices.

(9) In the light of the historical evidence these forms of "co-operation" of church and state in education are actually examples of "an establishment of religion" and as such are unconstitutional.

(10) The principle of separation of church and state requires that our federal and state governments shall rest upon the common decisions made freely by persons of all faiths without distinguishing among religious preferences and without insisting upon religious sanctions. To this end the public school system was created and designed to promote the common values of democratic citizenship among all people without regard to religious preferences or any supporting religious sanctions. Only in this way was it felt by the public school founders that religious freedom and equal rights of conscience could be fully protected for all, and only in this way was it felt by the founders of the Republic that the civil community could rest upon secure, peaceful, and democratic foundations.

To all who accept the historic meaning of the separation of church and state as described in these pages and as summarized above, it must be clear that present day practices should be examined in the light of this history and that present day policies should be made with clear understanding of this history. To be sure, we have every right to make common decisions for change in our historic traditions, but the choices before us cannot wisely be made without regard to the traditions that live on in us and the reasons that led to the making of the tradition.

The question the American people must now face is whether or not they wish to make decisions that are based upon this history. Shall we make decisions in conformity with this tradition of separation of church and state? Or shall we, for reasons of weight, depart from this tradition? If we decide to return to some form of "co-operation" between church and state (as defined in alternative 3b on page 8), we must take responsibility for realizing that we are returning to some form of "an establishment of religion" and we must be prepared for the consequences. We must remember that efforts to maintain or restore establishments of religion in the past have stimulated divisive forces in the American community and have likewise created the risk of increasing state control over religion.

The American people must now consider carefully whether or not such a return would become a threat to genuine freedom of religion based upon equal rights of conscience, a threat which the founding fathers so clearly saw when they framed the First Amendment to the United States Constitution. They saw that the best protection for religious freedom was to make questions of public policy a matter for common decision among people of all faiths without regard to religious sanctions or lack of them. They therefore took the fourth choice now before us (see page 9), the principle of separation of church and state. They decided that the government of the United States must rest upon the common decisions of the widest possible community. Only in this way could freedom of religion rest upon secure foundations; only in this way could "We the people" be fully free "to form a more perfect Union, establish Justice, insure domestic Tranquility, provide for the common defence, promote the general Welfare, and secure the Blessings of Liberty to ourselves and our Posterity."

The American people are now being required to decide once again whether or not this historic principle of separation of church and state is an indispensable element in deciding questions of public policy especially as they apply to education. Wise judgments concerning public policy, now as in the past, should rest upon sound historical interpretations of the origin and meaning of our traditions for us. To the making of wise decisions on the critical issues of church and state in American education, this brief study of our history has been dedicated.

Notes

Chapter 1.

THE CHOICES BEFORE US

1. Everson v. Board of Education 330 U.S. 1 (1947); and McCollum v. Board of Education of School District No. 71, Champaign County, Ill., 333 U.S. 203 (1948).
2. See, for example, Wilfred Parsons, *The First Freedom* (The Declan X. McMullen C., New York, 1948); *Christianity and Crisis*, Vol. VIII, No. 12 (July 5, 1948), pp. 1-2; Council for Social Action of the Congregational Christian Churches, *Social Action*, Vol. XIV, No. 9 (Nov. 15, 1948), pp. 30-39; statement of the Administrative Board of the National Catholic Welfare Conference, "The Christian in Action," published in *The New York Times* (Sunday, November 21, 1948), p. 63; and J. M. O'Neill, *Religion and Education under the Constitution* (Harper and Brothers, New York, 1949).

Chapter 2.

WHAT "ESTABLISHMENT OF RELIGION" MEANT IN COLONIAL AMERICA

1. Quoted in Columbia University, *Introduction to Contemporary Civilization in the West; A Source Book* (Columbia University Press, New York, 1946), I, 21-22.
2. Evarts B. Greene, *Religion and the State* (New York University Press, New York, 1941), p. 8.
3. For evidence concerning the establishment in Virginia, see H. J. Eckenrode, *Separation of Church and State in Virginia* (Virginia State Library, Special Report of the Department of Archives and History, Richmond, 1910), pp. 5-40.
4. Quoted in Columbia University, *Introduction to Contemporary Civilization in the West; A Source Book* (Columbia University Press, New York, 1946), I, 514, 515, 519-20.
5. Quoted in Louis M. Hacker, *The Shaping of the American Tradition* (Columbia University Press, New York, 1947), p. 108.
6. For a general summary of the development in New York, see Sanford H. Cobb, *The Rise of Religious Liberty in America* (Macmillan, New York, 1902), pp. 303 ff.
7. F. N. Thorpe, *The Federal and State Constitutions, Colonial Charters, and Other Organic Laws* (Government Printing Office, Washington, D. C. 1909), p. 2636. [Italics added]

8. *Acts and Resolves of Province of Massachusetts Bay*, I, 62. For details of the Massachusetts establishment, see Paul E. Lauer, *Church and State in New England* (Johns Hopkins University Studies in Historical and Political Science, Tenth Series, The Johns Hopkins University Press, Baltimore, 1892), and Jacob C. Meyer, *Church and State in Massachusetts from 1740 to 1833* (Western Reserve University Press, Cleveland, 1930).

9. Thorpe, *op. cit.*, pp. 1889-1890.

10. For details of the Connecticut establishment, see M. Louise Green, *The Development of Religious Liberty in Connecticut* (Houghton Mifflin, Boston, 1905).

11. *Acts and Laws of the State of Connecticut in America* (New London, 1784). See especially the sections on Conscience, pp. 21-22; Ministers, pp. 157-160; and Ecclesiastical Societies, pp. 235-237.

12. F. N. Thorpe, *The Federal and State Constitutions, Colonial Charters and Other Organic Laws* (Government Printing Office, Washington, D. C., 1909), p. 1689. [Italics added]

13. *Ibid.*, p. 1705. [Italics added]

14. *Ibid.*, pp. 3255-3256. [Italics added]

Chapter 3.

THE PRINCIPLE OF SEPARATION IN THE ORIGINAL STATES

1. Gaillard Hunt (ed.), *The Writings of James Madison* (G. P. Putnam's Sons, New York, 1900), I, 40.

2. *Ibid.*, p. 41, note. For a full discussion of the Virginia convention and Madison's part in it, see Irving Brant, *James Madison; The Virginia Revolutionist* (Bobbs-Merrill Co., Indianapolis, 1941), Chapter XII.

3. Thorpe, *op. cit.*, p. 3814.

4. Saul K. Padover, *The Complete Jefferson* (Duell, Sloan & Pearce, New York, 1943), p. 109; see also P. L. Ford, *The Works of Thomas Jefferson* (G. P. Putnam's Sons, New York, 1904), II, 180. [Italics added]

5. Dumas Malone, *Jefferson the Virginian* (Little, Brown, Boston, 1948), p. 275.

6. For details see H. J. Eckenrode, *Separation of Church and State in Virginia* (A Special Report of Department of Archives and History, Virginia State Library, Richmond, 1910), pp. 41-53.

7. W. W. Hening, *Laws of Virginia, Statutes at Large* (Richmond, 1823), XII, 84-86. [Italics added]

8. Eckenrode, *op. cit.*, pp. 58-61.

9. There was, for example, very close similarity between this bill and the provisions of Chapter 38 of the Constitution of South Carolina adopted in 1778. See the text in F. N. Thorpe, *The Federal and State Constitutions, Colonial Charters and Other Organic Laws* (Government Printing Office, Washington, 1909), VI, 3255-3257.

10. Eckenrode, *op. cit.*, pp. 58-59. [Italics added]

11. See Padover, *op. cit.*, 673-676; also Ford, *op. cit.*, IV, 74-82.

12. Padover, *op. cit.*, p. 113; also Ford, *op. cit.*, IV, 154. [Italics added]

13. Eckenrode, *op. cit.,* p. 86. [Italics added]
14. *Washington Mss.* (Papers of George Washington, Vol. 231), Library of Congress. The assessment bill is quoted in full in the supplemental appendix of the Supreme Court decision, Everson v. Board of Education, 330 U. S. 1.
15. Eckenrode, *op. cit.,* pp. 85-86.
16. Irving Brant, *James Madison; the Nationalist* .(Bobbs-Merrill, Indianapolis, 1948), p. 347.
17. Reported in detail in Eckenrode, *op. cit.,* pp. 86-114.
18. Gaillard Hunt, *The Writings of James Madison* (G. P. Putnam's Sons, New York, 1901), II, 183-191.
19. *Ibid.,* pp. 184-185.
20. *Ibid.,* p. 186.
21. *Ibid.,* p. 186. [Italics Madison's]
22. *Ibid.,* p. 187.
23. In a letter to Madison from Paris on February 8, 1786, Jefferson stated, "I thank you for the communication of the remonstrance against the assessment . . . . It will do us great honour. I wish it may be as much approved by our assembly as by the wisest part of Europe." Ford, *op. cit.,* V, 78.
24. For Jefferson's later comments on the struggles for religious freedom in Virginia, see Padover, *op. cit.,* pp. 285, 1147, 1288, 1295.
25. John C. Fitzpatrick, ed., *The Writings of George Washington* (U. S. Government Printing Office, Washington, D. C., 1939), XXVIII, 285.
26. See Thorpe, *op. cit.,* as follows: Delaware, pp. 567-568; Georgia, pp. 784-789, 800-801; New Jersey, pp. 2597-2598; New York, pp. 2636-2637; North Carolina, p. 2793; Pennsylvania, pp. 3082, 3100; Rhode Island, pp. 3213, 3222-3223; South Carolina, pp. 3257, 3264; and Virginia, p. 3814.
27. See *Ibid.,* as follows: Connecticut pp. 544-5; Maryland, pp. 1689-1690, 1705; Massachusetts, pp. 1889-1890, 1914; and New Hampshire, pp. 2453, 2493.

Chapter 4.

THE PRINCIPLE OF SEPARATION IN THE NATION

1. Quoted in Edward Frank Humphrey, *Nationalism and Religion in America 1774-1789* (Chipman Law Publishing Co., Boston, 1924), p. 432.
2. P. J. Treat, *The National Land System* (E. B. Treat & Co., New York, 1910), p. 36. The motion on the religious clause was put in such way that a majority was not obtained for keeping the clause, whereas it might have been retained if the motion had been put in another way.
3. Gaillard Hunt (ed.), *Writings of James Madison,* II, 145. (Letter to James Monroe, May 29, 1785.)
4. George W. Knight, *History and Management of Land Grants for Education In the Northwest Territory* (Papers of the American Historical Association, Vol. I, No. 3, G. P. Putnam's Sons, 1885), p. 18.
5. E. H. Scott (ed.), *Journal of the Constitutional Convention* (kept by James Madison), (Albert Scott & Co., Chicago, 1893), p. 69.
6. See Max Farrand (ed.), *The Records of the Federal Convention*

(Yale University Press, New Haven, 1911), Vol. III, Appendix. Hamilton's plan also contained a section on religion, but his plan was not considered by the Convention, p. 628. The plan debated by the Convention was submitted by Edmund Randolph, but it contained no reference to religion.

7. Ford, *op. cit.,* V, 371-372. [Italics added]

8. Gaillard Hunt (ed.), *The Writings of James Madison* (G. P. Putnam's Sons, New York, 1904) V, 271-272. [Italics added] The Mr. Wilson referred to was James Wilson of Pennsylvania who had fought Pennsylvania's democratic constitution of 1776 and took the leadership in rewriting Pennsylvania's more conservative Constitution of 1790.

9. *Ibid.,* V, 273.

10. *Ibid.,* V, 320. [Italics added]

11. Ford, *op. cit.,* V, 461-464.

12. Herman V. Ames, *The Proposed Amendments to the Constitution of the United States during the First Hundred Years of its History* (Annual Report of the American Historical Association for the Year 1896, Government Printing Office, Washington, D. C., 1897), p. 183. Seven of the states had proposed 124 articles of amendment at the time of debating adoption of the constitution: Massachusetts, 9; South Carolina, 4; New Hampshire, 12; Virginia, 20; New York, 32; North Carolina, 26; and Rhode Island, 21.

13. Joseph Gales (ed.), *Annals of Congress* (Gales & Seaton, Washington, D. C., 1834), I, 451. (Madison's entire speech of June 8 is also contained in Hunt, *op. cit.,* V, 370-389. In a footnote on p. 389 Hunt prints Madison's notes for this speech. In one section of the notes appear the words "Bill of Rights—useful not essential." Careful study of the speech reveals that this phrase refers to his earlier questions about the limited value of paper statements or "parchment barriers" in the face of determined majorities, as well as to the English experience and success in protecting rights without a written constitution. But the whole effect of the speech itself was to stress the necessity of a bill of rights now that the Constitution had been adopted by eleven states.)

14. *Ibid.,* p. 452. Madison sent to Jefferson in Paris his whole list of proposed amendments as proposed in his speech of June 8. Jefferson commented on the list in his letter to Madison of August 28, 1789: "I like it as far as it goes, but I should have been for going further." Ford, *op. cit.,* V, 492. Jefferson then wrote out detailed suggestions for additions or alterations of all those articles which he wanted to see changed. He did not mention either article on religion and thus presumably approved the limitation upon the states as well as upon Congress.

15. *Ibid.,* pp. 454-455.

16. This view had been elaborated by Madison in a long letter to Jefferson written on October 24, 1787, when he had sent Jefferson a copy of the newly framed constitution. In this letter Madison said, "A constitutional negative on the laws of the States seems equally necessary to secure individuals agst. encroachments on their rights." Hunt, *op. cit.,* V, 27. On pages 27-31 Madison expands on the meaning of this for a society divided into many religious sects.

17. Gales, *op. cit.,* p. 457. Madison's view of the role of the courts as pro-

tectors of the civil rights of the people against infringement by the legislative branches of government is interesting in view of recent attacks upon the Supreme Court as a usurper of the legislative function. See, for example, J. M. O'Neill, *Religion and Education under the Constitution* (Harper and Brothers, New York, 1949).

18. Gales, *op. cit.*, p. 458. All states had declarations in favor of religious freedom, but, as we have seen, five states still allowed multiple establishments. So Madison must have been referring to establishment when he said, "I know, in some of the State constitutions, the power of the government is controlled by such a declaration; but others are not."
19. *Ibid.*, p. 757.
20. *Ibid.*, pp. 757-8.
21. *Ibid.*, p. 759. This wording followed the proposal for amendment made by the New Hampshire convention when it ratified the Constitution. It might be interpreted to mean that Congress could not touch the establishments still existing in some of the states, notably New Hampshire. We do not know how Madison voted on this wording nor his attitude to it, but it was not in conformity with Madison's earlier proposals nor with the wording as finally adopted by the House on August 20.
22. *Ibid.*, p. 784.
23. *Ibid.*, p. 796. This wording returned substantially to the meaning of Madison's original proposal; if anything, it was broader in its application.
24. *Journal of the House of Representatives of the United States* (Printed by Francis Childs and John Swaine, New York, 1789), p. 107. The discrepancy between the wording of the *Annals* and the *Journal* may reveal minor changes for grammatical purposes.
25. *Ibid.*, p. 108. For some reason Livermore's revision of wording was not retained.
26. *Journal of the First Session of the Senate of the United States of America* (Printed by Thomas Greenleaf, New York, 1789), pp. 103-106.
27. *Ibid.*, p. 116.
28. *Ibid.*, p. 117.
29. *Ibid.*, p. 117.
30. *Ibid.*, p. 129.
31. *House Journal, op. cit.*, p. 146.
32. *Senate Journal, op. cit.*, pp. 141-142.
33. *House Journal, op. cit.*, p. 151.
34. *Senate Journal, op. cit.*, p. 145.
35. *Senate Journal, op. cit.*, p. 145; also *House Journal, op. cit.*, p. 152.
36. *Senate Journal, op. cit.*, pp. 150-151. When the twelve proposed articles of amendment were proposed to the states, the first two were not ratified, and thus the third article became the First Amendment.
37. Ames, *op. cit.*, p. 183. "In many of the States opposition to the ratification of the Constitution was based upon the absence of specific reservation of the rights of the people. The precedents of the great English declaratory statutes had been followed in the elaborate Bill of Rights which prefaced most of the State constitu-

tions." The people did not feel secure in their liberties without written guarantees to protect them from encroachment by the general government as well as by the state governments.

38. *U. S. Statutes at Large,* Foreign treaties, VIII, 155.
39. Padover, *op. cit.,* pp. 518-519; H. A. Washington (ed.), *The Writings of Thomas Jefferson* (Taylor & Maury, Washington, D. C., 1854), VIII, 113.
40. Ford, *op. cit.,* IX, 346-347. [Italics added]
41. Padover, *op. cit.,* p. 412; see also Ford, *op. cit.,* X, 131. Madison would have made the last clause read ". . . under the direction or discipline acknowledged within the several states." This wording would have acknowledged no right of the state authorities to have direction or discipline over religious societies. Ford, *op. cit.,* X, 128.
42. Ford, *op. cit.,* XI, 7-9.
43. See letters to Methodists of Pittsburgh and New London, Padover, *op. cit.,* pp. 541, 544; Washington, *op. cit.,* VIII, 142-143, 144-145.
44. James D. Richardson, *A Compilation of the Messages and Papers of the Presidents* (Government Printing Office, Washington, D. C., 1896), I, 490.
45. *Ibid.,* p. 490. [Italics added]
46. Elizabeth Fleet (ed.), "Madison's 'Detached Memoranda'" in *The William and Mary Quarterly,* Third Series, Vol. III, No. 4, October, 1946, p. 555. [Italics added]
47. *Ibid.,* pp. 558-559. [Italics added]
48. *Ibid.,* pp. 560-561. [Italics Madison's]
49. Hunt, *op. cit.,* IX, 100-103. [Abbreviations have been written out.]
50. T. M. Cooley, *A Treatise on the Constitutional Limitations. . .* Little, Brown & Co., Boston, 1927), Vol. II, Chap. XIII, "On Religious Liberty," pp. 966-969. For a convenient and easily available summary of constitutional provisions relating to separation of church and state, see National Education Association, *Research Bulletin,* "The State and Sectarian Education," Vol. XXIV, No. 1, February, 1946.
51. Thorpe, *op. cit.,* p. 981. Article VIII, sec. 3. [Italics added]
52. N.E.A., *Research Bulletin, op. cit.,* p. 9.
53. Herman V. Ames, *The Proposed Amendments to the Constitution of the United States during the First Hundred Years of its History* (Annual Report of the American Historical Association for the Year 1896, Government Printing Office, Washington, D. C., 1897), p. 175.
54. Gitlow v. New York, 268 U.S. 652 (1925), p. 666.
55. See, for example, Cantwell v. Connecticut, 310 U.S. 296; Minersville School District v. Gobitis, 310 U.S. 586; Jamison v. Texas, 318 U.S. 413; Sargent v. Texas, 318 U.S. 418; Murdock v. Pennsylvania, 319 U.S. 105; West Virginia State Board of Education v. Barnette, 319 U.S. 624; Prince v. Massachusetts, 321 U.S. 158; Follett v. McCormick, 321 U.S. 573; Thomas v. Collins, 323 U.S. 516, 530; Marsh v. Alabama, 327 U.S. 501.
56. Everson v. Board of Education, 330 U.S. 1, pp. 15-16. [Italics added]
57. This is *not* to argue that the *practical* ruling of the majority in the Everson case was in accordance with the *principle* as set forth therein and as quoted above.

Chapter 5.

THE MEANING OF SEPARATION FOR EDUCATION IN THE
NINETEENTH CENTURY

1. See Robert F. Seybolt, *Source Studies in American Colonial Education: The Private School* (University of Illinois Press, Urbana, 1925).
2. For example, New York State passed a general common school law for New York City on May 7, 1844, in which it was provided that no religious instruction should be given which could be construed to violate the rights of conscience "as secured by the Constitution of the state and of the United States." Here is direct appeal to the First Amendment *before* the Fourteenth Amendment. Laws of New York, 1844, Ch. 300, Sec. 12.
3. See, for example, J. M. O'Neill, *Religion and Education under the Constitution* (Harper, New York, 1949), pp. 76-77.
4. See, for example, Roy J. Honeywell, *The Educational Work of Thomas Jefferson* (Harvard University Press, Cambridge, 1931) and Philip Alexander Bruce, *History of the University of Virginia* (Macmillan, New York, 1920), 2 vols.
5. Padover, *op. cit.,* p. 1049; and Ford, *op. cit.,* II, 417.
6. Padover, *op. cit.,* p. 667; also Ford, *op. cit.,* IV, 62.
7. Padover, *op. cit.,* pp. 667, 1052; Ford, *op. cit.,* II, 423.
8. Padover, *op. cit.,* 1072; Honeywell, *op. cit.,* p. 233; Washington, *op. cit.,* IX, 490.
9. Padover, *op. cit.,* p. 1076; Honeywell, *op. cit.,* p. 235; Washington, *op. cit.,* IX, 495.
10. Honeywell, *op. cit.,* pp. 207, 209; Ford, *op. cit.,* IV, 431, 434.
11. Malone, *op. cit.,* p. 285.
12. Padover, *op. cit.,* pp. 669-670; Ford, *op. cit.,* IV, 66-67. [Italics added]
13. Padover, *op. cit.,* pp. 1064-1069; Honeywell, *op. cit.,* pp. 222-227.
14. Padover, *op. cit.,* pp. 1078, 1082; Honeywell, *op. cit.,* pp. 238, 241.
15. Honeywell, *op. cit.,* pp. 250, 252-253; Padover, *op. cit.,* pp. 1098, 1100-1101.
16. Honeywell, *op. cit.,* p. 256; Padover, *op. cit.,* p. 1104.
17. Honeywell, *op. cit.,* p. 256; Padover, *op. cit.,* p. 1104.
18. Padover, *op. cit.* pp. 957-958; Andrew A. Lipscomb (ed.) *The Writings of Thomas Jefferson* (Thomas Jefferson Memorial Association, Washington, D. C. 1903), XIX, 414-416. [Italics added]
19. Ford, *op. cit.,* XI, 272. [Italics added]
20. Padover, *op. cit.,* p. 110; Honeywell, *op. cit.,* pp. 274-275; Lipscomb, *op. cit.,* XIX, 449. [Italics added] It is interesting to note that Webster defines "precincts" in the plural as "the region immediately surrounding a place."
21. P. A. Bruce, *History of the University of Virginia* (Macmillan, New York, 1920) II, 367-369. [Italics added]
22. *Ibid.,* II, 368.
22a. Honeywell, *op. cit.,* p. 249.
22b. *Ibid.,* p. 275.
22c. Jefferson Papers, Library of Congress, vol. 229, Folio 40962. Columbia

University Library, Microfilm, Reel 93, includes Jefferson Papers, Vols. 229-230, Folios 40901-41280 (March 13 to December 30, 1825).

23. Bruce, *op. cit.,* II, 370. [Italics added]
24. *Laws of Massachusetts,* 1827, Ch. 143, Sec. 7.
25. Massachusetts constitution, eighteenth amendment, adopted in 1855, see Thorpe, *op. cit.,* p. 1918.
26. Jenkins v. Andover, 103 Mass. 94 (1869).
27. See Thorpe, *op. cit.,* Wisconsin (1848), Art I, sec. 18, pp. 4078-4079; Michigan (1850), Art. 4, sec. 40, p. 1950; Indiana (1851), Art. 1, sec. 6, p. 1074; Oregon (1857), Art 1, sec. 5, p. 2998; and Minnesota (1857), Art 1, sec. 16, p. 1993.
28. Laws of New York, 1812-13, Ch. LII, Sec. IV.
29. See *Minutes of the Public School Society* (mss. records at the New York Historical Society), Aug. 1, 1834.
30. See *The Important and Interesting Debate, On the Claim of the Catholics to a Portion of the Common School Fund; With the Arguments of Council, Before the Board of Aldermen of the City of New-York, on Thursday and Friday, the 29th and 30th of October, 1840.* (Second Ed., published by the Proprietor of the New-York Freeman's Journal)
31. *Ibid.*
32. Board of Alderman of the City of New York, Document No. 40, 1841, p. 557.
33. *Laws of New York,* 1842, 65th Session, Ch. 150. 14.
34. People v. Board of Education, 13 Barb. 400 (New York, 1851) pp. 408-411.
35. Henry Stephens Randall, *Decision of the State Superintendent of Common Schools, on the Right to Compel Catholic Children to Attend Prayers, and to Read or Commit Portions of the Bible, as School Exercises* (Department of Common Schools, Albany, Oct. 27, 1853), pp. 5-8. [Italics added]
36. For convenient summaries of constitutional and statutory prohibitions, see Carl Zollman, *Church and School in the American Law* (Concordia Publishing House, St. Louis, Mo., 1918) and N.E.A. Research Bulletin, *The State and Sectarian Education* (Feb., 1946).
37. Board of Education v. Minor, 23 Ohio 211 (1872), p. 211.
38. Article I, Sec. 7 of Ohio constitution, see *ibid.,* p. 241.
39. *Ibid.,* pp. 248-251. [Italics the court's]
40. *Ibid.,* pp. 253-254.
41. For summaries of specific states, see Zollman, *op. cit.,* and N.E.A. Research Bulletin, *op. cit.*
42. Thorpe, *op. cit.,* p. 1035, Illinois constitution, Article 8, Sec. 3 (1870).
43. Quoted in *Catholic World,* 22: 434-435 (January 1876). In commenting on the speech, the editor says, ". . . We agree with the President: 1st no 'sectarianism' in our common schools; and, therefore, 'not one dollar' to our present system of schools, because they are sectarian" (p. 440).
44. Richardson, *op. cit.,* VII, 332-356. Grant also proposed that tax exemption for church property should be removed and all property, whether church or corporation, should be taxed. Grant urged that the church and state be declared forever separate and distinct.

45. House Resolution 1, 44th Congress, 1st Sess. (1876), *Congressional Record,* V. 4, Part 6, p. 5453.
46. Quoted in Zollman, *op. cit.,* p. 8. The Republican platform of 1880 carried another such plank.
47. Herman V. Ames, *The Proposed Amendments to the Constitution of the United States during the First Century of its History,* Annual Report of the American Historical Association for the year 1896 (Government Printing Office, Washington, D. C., 1897), pp. 275-278. Ames comments: "The provisions of the State constitutions are in almost all instances adequate on this subject, and no amendment is likely to be secured" (p. 278).
48. See for example, Thorpe, *op. cit.,* p. 2964 for Oklahoma, New Mexico and Arizona. Other states were Montana, Nevada, North Dakota, South Dakota, Utah, Washington, and Wyoming; see Zollman, *op. cit.* pp. 9-10.
49. See Gordon Canfield Lee, *The Struggle for Federal Aid, First Phase; A History of the Attempts to Obtain Federal Aid for the Common Schools, 1870-1890* (Teachers College Bureau of Publications, New York, 1949), pp. 46-47, 69-70, and 118-123.
50. Alvin W. Johnson, *The Legal Status of Church-State Relationships in the United States* (University of Minnesota Press, Minneapolis, 1934), p. 23.
51. U.S. *Statutes at Large,* 29: 411 (June 11, 1896). See also 29: 683 (March 3, 1897); 29: 345 (June 10, 1896); 30: 97 (June 7, 1897); 39:988 (March 2, 1917).
52. U.S. *Statutes at Large,* 39: 936 (Feb. 23, 1917). [Italics added]

Chapter 6.

THE STRUGGLE FOR SEPARATION IN EDUCATION IN THE
TWENTIETH CENTURY

1. For detailed summaries of these issues by states, see Johnson, Alvin W. and Yost, Frank H., *Separation of Church and State in the United States* (University of Minnesota Press, Minneapolis, 1948), Chapters VII, IX, XII, and XIII; and N.E.A., *Research Bulletin,* "The State and Sectarian Education," (February, 1946), pp. 14-24.
2. These statistics are based upon a comprehensive study made at the University of Wisconsin at the time of a referendum in the state of Wisconsin on the bus issue: *A Guide Relating to School Transportation in Wisconsin* (mimeographed), University Extension Division, Department of Debating and Public Discussion (Madison, Wisconsin, August, 1946).
3. State ex rel. Van Straten v. Milquet, 192 N.W. 392, (Wis. 1923) p. 395. [Italics added]
4. State ex rel. Traub et al. v. Brown, 172 Atl. 835 (Del. 1934) p. 837. [Italics added]
5. Judd et al. v. Board of Education of Union Free School Dist. No. 2, Town of Hempstead, Nassau County, et al., 15 N.E. (2d) 576 (N.Y. 1938), pp. 581-582. [Italics added]
6. *Ibid.,* p. 582.

7. Gurney et al. v. Ferguson et al., 122 Pac. (2d) 1002 (Okla. 1942) p. 1004.
8. Synopsis 7 in Sherrard v. Jefferson County Board of Education et al., 171 S.W. (2d) 963 (Ky. 1942). [Italics added]
9. *Ibid.,* p. 968.
10. Mitchell v. Consolidated School District No. 201 et al., 135 Pac. (2d) 79 (Wash. 1943), pp. 81-82. [Italics added]
11. Board of Education of Baltimore County v. Wheat, 199 Atl. 628 (Md. 1938), p. 632.
12. Nichols et al. v. Henry, 191 S.W. (2d) 930 (Ky. 1945) p. 932. [Italics added]
13. *Ibid.,* p. 935. [Italics added]
14. Bowker v. Baker et al., 167 Pac. (2d) 256 (Calif. 1946) p. 261. [Italics added]
15. Everson v. Board of Education, 330 U.S. 1 (1947) pp. 15-16. [Italics added]
16. *Ibid.,* pp. 16-18. [Italics added]
17. *Ibid.,* pp. 29, 31-32, 33. [Italics added]
18. *Ibid.,* pp. 44-50, 57.
19. *Ibid.,* pp. 58-59. [Italics added]
20. *Ibid.,* pp. 59-60. [Italics added]
21. *Ibid.,* pp. 24, 25, 26, 27, 27-28. [Italics added]
22. Silver Lake Consolidated School District v. Parker et al., 29 N. W. (2d) 214 (Iowa 1947), p. 219
23. Visser v. Nooksack Valley School Dist. No. 506, Whatcom County, et al., 207 Pac. 204-5 (Washington, 1949).
24. Smith v. Donahue et al., 195 N. Y. S. 715 (1922), pp. 721-722. [Italics added]
25. Cochran v. La. State Bd. of Ed., 281 U. S. 370 (1930), pp. 374-375. [Italics added]
26. *Ibid.,* p. 375. [Italics added]
27. Everson v. Bd. of Ed., 330 U. S. 1 (1947), footnote #42 on p. 50.
28. Chance v. Mississippi State Textbook Rating and Purchasing Board, 200 So. 706 (1941), p. 710. [Italics added]
29. See William A. Mitchell, "Religion and Federal Aid to Education," in School of Law, Duke University, *Law and Contemporary Problems,* issue entitled "Religion and the State" (Winter, 1949), XIV, 113-143.
30. The National School Lunch Act as passed on June 4, 1946 provides that federal funds may be allocated directly to non-public schools in those 27 states which do not disburse funds for free lunches to private and parochial school children. The new school lunch program of 1948 carries the following formula:

  If, in any State, the State educational agency is not permitted by law to disburse the funds paid to it under this chapter to non-profit private schools in the State, or is not permitted by law to match federal funds made available for use by such nonprofit private schools, the Secretary [of Agriculture] shall withhold from the funds apportioned to any such State under sections 1753 and 1754 of this title the same proportion of the funds as the number of children between the ages of five and seventeen, inclusive, attending nonprofit private schools within the State is of the total number of persons of those ages within the State attending school. The Secretary shall disburse the funds so withheld directly to the nonprofit private schools within said State for the same purpose and subject to the same conditions as are authorized or required with respect to the disbursements to schools within the State by the State educational agency, including the requirement that any such payment or payments shall be matched, in the proportion specified in section 1756 of this title for such State, by funds from sources within the State expended by nonprofit private schools within the State participating in the school-lunch program under this chapter. Such funds shall not be considered a part of the funds constituting the matching funds under the terms of section 1756 of this title.

See U. S. Code Annotated (1948), Chapter 13, Title 42, Section 1759, p. 337.

31. Williams et al. v. Board of Trustees Stanton Common School Dist., 191 S. W. 507 (Ky. 1917), p. 512.
32. N. E. A., *Research Bulletin,* "The State and Sectarian Education" (February, 1946), pp. 17-20, and 36.
33. Williams v. Board of Trustees, 191 S. W. 507 (Ky. 1917), p. 513.
34. Knowlton v. Baumhover, 166 N. W. 202 (Iowa 1918), p. 204.
35. *Ibid.,* p. 205.
36. *Ibid.,* pp. 206-207.
37. Harfst et al. v. Hoegen et al., 163 S. W. (2d) 609 (Mo. 1941), p. 613.
38. See National Commission for the Defense of Democracy through Education of the National Education Association, Report of an Investigation, *North College Hill, Ohio, An Example of Some Effects of Board of Education Interference with Sound Administration of Public Education* (November, 1947), 30 pp.
39. *Ibid.,* pp. 10-11.
40. *Ibid.,* pp. 20-21.
41. Zellers v. Huff, District Court, First Judicial District, State of New Mexico, County of Sante Fe, Declaratory Judgment, March 12, 1949.
42. For detailed summaries of the issue by states, see Johnson, Alvin W. and Yost, Frank H., *Separation of Church and State in the United States* (University of Minnesota Press, Minneapolis, 1948), Chapters III, IV, V, and VIII; and N.E.A., *Research Bulletin,* "The State and Sectarian Education," (February, 1946), pp. 24-30.
43. Thorpe, *op. cit.,* p. 4136.
44. N. E. A., *Research Bulletin, op. cit.,* pp. 34, 36.
45. For summaries of many such cases, see Johnson and Yost, *op. cit.,* Chapter IV, especially with regard to decisions in Colorado, Georgia, Iowa, Kansas, Kentucky, Maine, Massachusetts, Michigan, Minnesota, Nebraska, New York, Ohio, Pennsylvania, and Texas.
46. Wilkerson v. City of Rome, 152 Ga. 652 (1921), pp. 773-774.
47. *Ibid.,* p. 786.
48. Pfeiffer v. Board of Education of Detroit, 118 Mich. 560 (1898), p. 572.

49. Kaplan v. Independent School Dist. of Virginia, et al., 214 N. W. 18 (Minn. 1927), pp. 22-23.
50. State v. District Board of School Dist. No. 8 of Edgerton, 44 N. W. 967 (Wis. 1890), p. 975.
51. People v. Board of Education of Dist. 24, 92 N. E. 251 (Ill. 1910), p. 255.
52. *Ibid.*, pp. 255-256.
53. Commonwealth v. Herr, 229 Pa. St. 132 (1910), p. 140.
54. *Ibid.*, p. 145.
55. O'Connor v. Hendrivk, 184 N. Y. 421 (1906), p. 428.
56. See *Journal of the National Education Association* (November, 1949), pp. 610-611. See also the complete report issued in June 1949.
57. Stein vs. Brown, 211 N.Y.S. 822 (1925), pp. 825-26.
58. Peoples vs. Graves, 219 N.Y.S. 189 (1927), pp. 194-195.
59. McCollum v. Board of Education, 330 U. S. 203 (1948), pp. 209-210. [Italics added]
60. *Ibid.*, pp. 211-212.
61. *Ibid.*, p. 213.
62. *Ibid.*, pp. 216-217. [Italics added]
63. *Ibid.*, pp. 227-228. [Italics added]
64. *Ibid.*, pp. 231-232. [Italics added]
65. Lewis v. Spaulding et al., 85 N. Y. S. (2d) 682 (1948), p. 686.
66. *Ibid.*, p. 687-88.
67. *Ibid.*, p. 689.
68. *Ibid.*, p. 690.
69. Balazs v. Board of Education of St. Louis, #18369, Div. No. 3, Circuit Court, St. Louis, Mo., May 25, 1948. A perpetual injunction was granted on November 22, 1948.
70. For an annotated bibliography of recent books, pamphlets, and articles up to August 1949 covering all points of view, see *Church, State and Education, A Selected Bibliography,* 15 mimeographed pages, compiled by the Library of Jewish Information, The American Jewish Committee, 386 Fourth Avenue, New York 16, N. Y.

Index

225